AN ANTHOLOGY OF Beetles

WARNING: This book is an introduction to the amazing world of beetles, and is for general information purposes only. Beetles play diverse and vital roles for healthy ecosystems, and we would not encourage beetle collection, as many beetle populations are declining and several beetles are protected by law. Please also be aware that touching some beetles may cause skin irritations or blisters.

AN ANTHOLOGY OF

Beetles

Written by Richard Jones
Illustrated by Angela Rizza
and Daniel Long

Contents

What are beetles? 6
Everyone knows a beetle 8
Feeding habits 10
Metamorphosis 12

WOODS AND FORESTS 14
Golden scarab beetle 15
Hercules beetle 16
Rainbow stag beetle 17
Titan longhorn 18
Violin beetle 19
Flat clown beetle 20
Beautiful carrion beetle 21
Bess beetle 22
Grant's stag beetle 23
Headlight beetle 24
Frog-legged beetle 25
Harlequin beetle 26
Spotted fungus beetle 27
Giraffe-necked weevil 28
Long-snouted weevil 29
Bright colours 30
Metallic weevil 32
Elm bark beetle 33
Rhinoceros beetle 34
Trilobite beetle 35
Conical fungus beetle 36
Black-headed cardinal beetle 37
Timberman 38
Scorpion longhorn 39

Mole beetle 40
Caterpillar hunter 41

FIELDS AND MEADOWS 42
Common claybank tiger beetle 43
Asian bombardier beetle 44
Narrow grass beetle 45
Featherwing beetle 46
Slender long-horned beetle 47
Masters of adaptation 48
Sacred scarab 50
Goliath beetle 51
Asian longhorn 52
Rice hispa 53
Thistle weevil 54
Minotaur beetle 55
Golden tortoise beetle 56
Glow-worm 57
Globe scarab beetle 58
Cicada parasite beetle 59
Golden-green pot beetle 60
Mushroom rove beetle 61
Thick-legged flower beetle 62
Cockchafer 63
Starburst chafer 64
Tufted jewel beetle 65
Willow flea beetle 66
Snail-killer beetle 67

PARKS AND GARDENS 68
- Seven-spot ladybird 69
- Net-winged beetle 70
- Great diving beetle 71
- Ten-lined June beetle 72
- Rose chafer 73
- Bee chafer 74
- Jewel beetle 75
- *Camouflage* 76
- Common eastern firefly 78
- Smooth spider beetle 79
- Horned fungus beetle 80
- Death-watch beetle 81
- Speckled oil beetle 82
- Alpine longhorn 83
- Coconut hispine 84
- Colorado potato beetle 85
- Bloody-nosed beetle 86
- Palm weevil 87
- Acorn weevil 88
- Whirligig beetle 89
- Devil's coach-horse 90
- Banded net-winged beetle 91
- Mealybug destroyer 92
- Tumbling flower beetle 93
- Musk beetle 94
- Cellar beetle 95

HARSH HABITATS 96
- Manticore beetle 97
- Sand beetle 98
- Bacon beetle 99
- Himalayan burying beetle 100
- Ant nest beetle 101
- Cave beetle 102
- House longhorn 103
- Sea lavender weevil 104
- Northern dune tiger beetle 105
- Poison arrow beetle 106
- Drugstore beetle 107
- Bumblebee rove beetle 108
- Bee beetle 109
- Wasp nest beetle 110
- Ironclad beetle 111
- Pie-dish beetle 112
- Wharf borer 113
- Grain weevil 114
- Green-footed peacock beetle 115
- Black fire beetle 116
- Red flour beetle 117
- Fighting tortoise beetle 118
- Reed beetle 119
- Fog-basking beetle 120
- Museum beetle 121
- *Conservation* 122

Glossary 124
Index 126
Acknowledgements 128

What are beetles?

Beetles are the largest group of insects and can be found on every continent except Antarctica. They belong to the order Coleoptera, which means "sheath-winged" in Greek. Beetles come in many colours, shapes, and sizes, but they all share some common features.

Wings

Beetles usually have two sets of wings. The hard pair, called wing cases, acts like a protective sheath for the two delicate flight wings. The wing cases flip open, but only the flexible rear wings flap up and down to power flights.

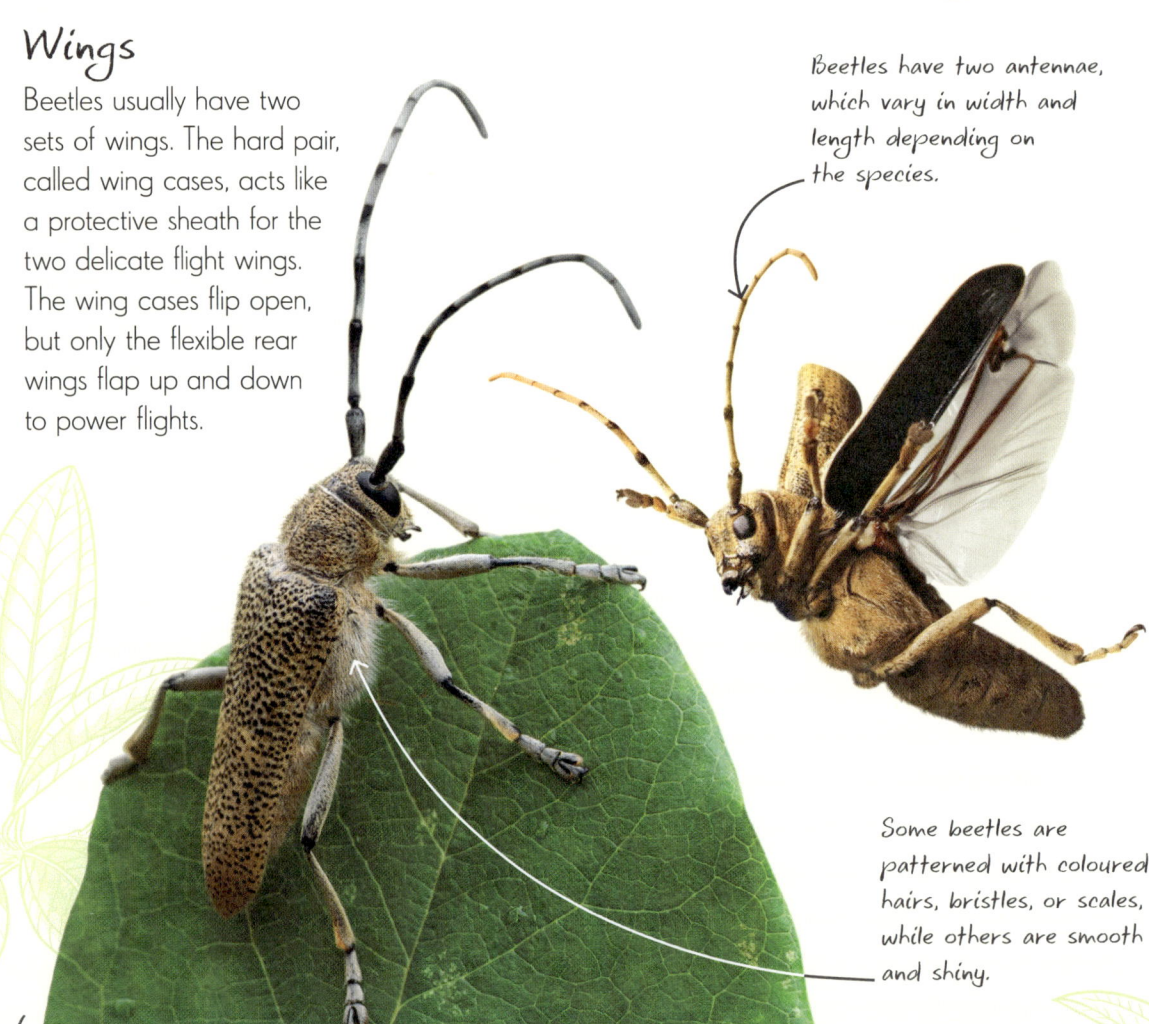

Beetles have two antennae, which vary in width and length depending on the species.

Some beetles are patterned with coloured hairs, bristles, or scales, while others are smooth and shiny.

Jaws

Beetles have two jaws that meet together like pliers or scissors. Some of them have long, curved jaws for fighting each other or for catching and eating other insects. Beetles with short, strong triangular jaws can chew tough plants and hard wood.

Larvae

These insects lay eggs that hatch into juvenile forms called larvae. Some young beetles have long legs and move about actively. Others, called grubs, are short and curved, with tiny, claw-like legs. A third kind, called maggots, have no legs at all.

The tiger beetle uses its dagger-like jaws to grasp small prey, such as insects.

Eyes

Most beetles have two eyes, usually positioned on the front of the head. However, some beetles that live underground, such as the narrow-necked cave beetle, have evolved without eyes.

Everyone knows a beetle

Beetles are found on every continent. They can get anywhere — from cracks in seaside rocks to high up on a hillside. These tough insects have lived on the Earth for millions of years and been a part of our stories for thousands. They've helped shape our environment — pollinating flowers and keeping pest numbers in check.

The twenty-two-spot ladybird always has 22 black spots on its body.

Like other insects, beetles like this false blister beetle help move pollen from flower to flower. This is called pollination and it helps plants grow new seeds.

Popular insects

Many of you may already know some beetles. Ladybirds are probably the most familiar of them all. They are easily recognized by their bright colours and spotted patterns. Other well-known beetles include fireflies, dung beetles, and weevils.

The harlequin ladybird can have up to 21 spots.

Ancient charm

Beetles have been known and loved for thousands of years. Ancient Egyptians considered the scarab beetle to be a good-luck charm. They made jewellery and giant stone sculptures shaped like these beetles.

A scarab amulet dating from ancient Egypt

Countless beetles

Beetles are one of the most diverse groups of animals on Earth. The smallest featherwings are only 0.3 mm (0.01 in) long, but giant longhorns can reach up to 170 mm (6.7 in). So far, about 400,000 different types have been identified, and many more are yet to be discovered.

The rhinoceros beetle is among the world's strongest insects.

Dogbane beetle

Varied diet

Not all beetles eat the same kind of food. The dogbane beetle, for example, feeds only on plants in the dogbane family, such as milkweed. Carpet beetle larvae chomp on wool and silk threads, which is how they get their name.

Carpet beetle larva

Feeding habits

Beetles and their larvae bite and chew using their two scissor- or plier-like jaws. Since many beetles eat plants, they often turn into pests of farm crops or garden flowers. In large numbers, beetles and their larvae can destroy whole fields of crops.

Crop raiders

Striped cucumber beetles are major crop pests in North America. They often spread wilt disease in plants, causing them to droop or die. These beetles consume plants from the gourd family, such as pumpkin and cucumber.

Drilling with snouts

Some beetles, such as weevils, have long snouts with small jaws at the tip. The snouts work like drills, cutting small, deep holes into plants. Then, the weevils use their long, flexible egg-laying tube to lay an egg inside. The grub grows up in hiding, feeding on the same plant.

The hazelnut weevil drills deep holes in hazelnuts with its snout.

Surprise feeding

Ground beetle larvae prey on small insects and grubs, as well as snails and spiders. Using their strong legs and smooth bodies, they push deep into leaf litter and grass roots. When prey passes by, they strike and kill it with their pointed jaws.

A ground beetle larva eating a snail.

Egg

A female Japanese beetle burrows into the soil to lay eggs in batches of one to five. Each egg is elliptical and about 1.55 mm (0.05 in) long. Within a week, the egg absorbs water from the soil, doubles in size, and becomes spherical.

The eggs can be translucent to pearly white.

Metamorphosis

Beetles don't look the same at every stage of life. They change a lot from the time they hatch out of a tiny egg. This transformation is called metamorphosis. The journey of a Japanese beetle is full of surprises. Starting with the female laying an egg underground, it grows into a shiny adult beetle over 1–2 years.

The larva can reach lengths of up to 32 mm (1.2 in).

Larva

The egg hatches into a larva, or grub. The juvenile spends most of its time eating and growing. Once the Japanese beetle larva has had enough food and reaches its full size, it stops feeding. Its skin then hardens into a tough, leathery pupa.

Adult

After a few weeks, the adult beetle emerges from the pupal case. Its length can range from 8–11 mm (0.3–0.4 in), often smaller than the fully grown larva.

The adult Japanese beetle is copper-green in colour.

The legs of the beetle are clearly visible in its pupa form.

Pupa

Inside the pupa, the larva's body breaks down into a nutrient-rich liquid. This helps form adult body parts, such as eyes, antennae, and wings. Although the beginnings of these features are present in a larva, they don't develop until it stops making a special chemical called juvenile hormone.

Woods and forests

With soft squishy leaves, rotting logs, and twisting, flower-laden trees, woodland offers a huge variety of homes for insects. Beetles can feed in the roots, under the bark, and deep inside the hard wood of trees. Some of them even dine on other bugs! Tropical rainforests have more beetles than anywhere else on Earth. In fact, nobody knows exactly how many there are — and scientists think there could be millions of undiscovered species in the world.

Golden scarab beetle

Chrysina resplendens

This scarab beetle looks as if it is made from polished gold, and its eye-catching appearance has a curious origin. The colour is not caused by pigments, but rather by the tiny grooves across its hard outer covering, or exoskeleton. The shape, size, and number of these grooves — only visible under powerful microscopes — split and scatter light, reflecting the gold.

Adult beetles are often spotted flying around at dusk.

Broad flat legs are ideal for digging in the leaf litter.

Location: Central America
Length: Up to 30 mm (1.2 in)

Hercules beetle

Dynastes hercules

Named after the mighty Greek hero, this super-strong beetle can lift nearly 2 kg (4 lbs) with its head — about 30 times its body weight. Only males have long horns, which they use to fight over females. They try to crush rivals between the horns on the head and thorax, often causing serious damage.

Its wing cases turn greenish-yellow in dry conditions and black when it's humid.

The horns on the thorax (above) and on the head (this one) clamp together like a claw.

Location: Central and South America
Length: Up to 170 mm (6.7 in)

Rainbow stag beetle

Phalacrognathus muelleri

These beautiful metallic insects are the largest stag beetles of Australia. The males use their unusual jaws to fight fiercely — attempting to flip their rivals off the log or tree trunk. In death, the wing cases fade to a dull brown, so pinned museum specimens never look as striking as the living insects.

The long, straight jaws are unique to this species.

Location: Northeast Australia
Length: Up to 75 mm (3 in)

Titan longhorn
Titanus giganteus

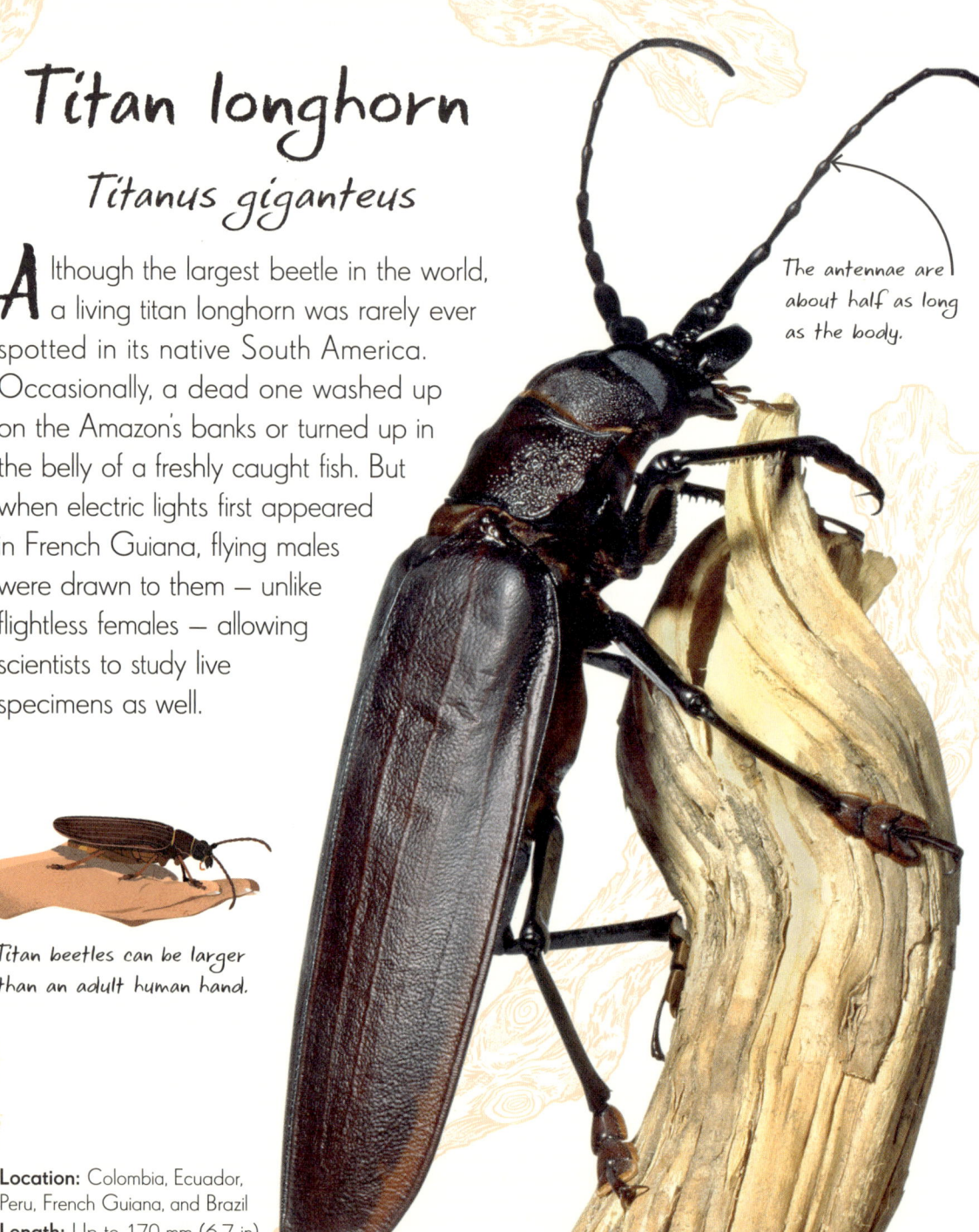

The antennae are about half as long as the body.

Although the largest beetle in the world, a living titan longhorn was rarely ever spotted in its native South America. Occasionally, a dead one washed up on the Amazon's banks or turned up in the belly of a freshly caught fish. But when electric lights first appeared in French Guiana, flying males were drawn to them — unlike flightless females — allowing scientists to study live specimens as well.

Titan beetles can be larger than an adult human hand.

Location: Colombia, Ecuador, Peru, French Guiana, and Brazil
Length: Up to 170 mm (6.7 in)

The wing cases are thin and slightly see-through.

Location: Malaysia, Borneo, and Indonesia
Length: Up to 90 mm (3.5 in)

Violin beetle

Mormolyce phyllodes

This beetle is actually very narrow, but the broad edges of its wing cases make it look like a dead leaf or flat seed. The larvae feed inside the hard fruiting bodies of bracket fungi, while adults prefer small insects. Its flat shape helps it slip under bark or between lobes of fungus.

The beetle is ten times wider than it is thick.

Short, sharp jaws

Location: Europe and northern Asia
Length: Up to 10 mm (0.39 in)

The last segment in the antenna is covered with sensory hairs.

Flat clown beetle

Hololepta plana

Small and flat, this beetle is incredibly tough. The flat clown beetle uses its compact shape and powerful, toothed legs to push its way under the bark of dead and decaying trees, especially poplars. Both adults and larvae eat small insects in rotting wood, particularly maggots.

Beautiful carrion beetle
Necrophila formosa

Carrion beetles are drawn to the smell of dead animals and often fly off in search of them. They feed on decaying flesh and fly maggots. Most carrion beetles are black, some with orange markings, but only this species has metallic blue wing cases. Its scientific name, *formosa*, means "beautiful".

A ridged back helps it slide under leaves or carrion.

The beetle uses its antennae to smell for food.

Location: Southeast Asia
Length: Up to 18 mm (0.7 in)

Bess beetle

Odontotaenius disjunctus

Bess beetles live in family groups under the rotting logs in which they feed. Both adults and larvae communicate by making squeaking sounds with their body parts. While the larvae rub their middle and back legs together, adults scrape the inside of the wing cases against the rough tip of their abdomen.

It has deep grooves on its wing cases.

Location: Eastern USA
Length: Up to 30 mm (1.2 in)

Long, curved jaws

Males use their plier-like mouthparts to grab each other during wrestling matches.

Location: South America
Length: Up to 90 mm (3.5 in)

Grant's stag beetle
Chiasognathus grantii

Only males of this species have long, antler-like jaws. Females have short, broad ones instead. The Grant's stag beetle made history in 1948 by appearing on Chile's 60-cent stamp — the first beetle ever to feature on a postage stamp.

In the Caribbean, these beetles are called "winkies" for their blinking lights.

Location: South America and Caribbean islands
Length: Up to 80 mm (3 in)

Headlight beetle
Pyrophorus noctilucus

This beetle has two small domed patches that produce the most brilliant light of any glowing insect — bright enough to read by. The glow comes from a reaction between the chemicals luciferin and luciferase, and is called "cold light" because it gives off no heat.

Though hard to miss due to its large size and striking colour, little is known about how this beetle lives.

Frog-legged beetle

Sagra buqueti

It's a bit of a mystery, but males of this unusual beetle likely use their huge, curved back legs to fight rivals. They may try to squeeze each other with these limbs, or perhaps females choose their mates based on leg size. Surprisingly, despite their name, they don't jump like frogs.

Back legs have a tuft of orange hairs.

Location: Southeast Asia
Length: Up to 13 mm (0.5 in)

Location: Central and South America
Length: Up to 80 mm (3 in)

Its front legs are longer than its body.

Harlequin beetle

Acrocinus longimanus

The males of this species have longer legs than females and use them to fight over mates and trees, where the females lay eggs. They try to hook and flip rivals off the trunk, but they must be careful. One bite from another harlequin beetle can break off a leg or antenna.

Location: India, China, and Southeast Asia
Length: Up to 13 mm (0.5 in)

Spotted fungus beetle
Eumorphus quadriguttatus

Fungus beetles mostly stay hidden under fallen logs, inside rotten wood, or beneath decaying bark. But many are brightly coloured, including some with spots like ladybirds. Their bold colours likely warn predators that they contain foul-tasting chemicals.

The spots can be of varying sizes and shapes.

Giraffe-necked weevil

Trachelophorus giraffa

These fascinating beetles are named for their elongated necks. Females use theirs to chew part way through a leaf, then roll it into a sausage shape to lay an egg inside. Males use their necks in gentle nodding contests, where the one with the longest neck warns off rivals without a fight or injury.

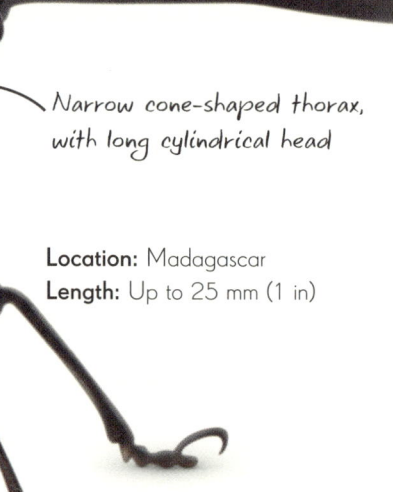

Narrow cone-shaped thorax, with long cylindrical head

Location: Madagascar
Length: Up to 25 mm (1 in)

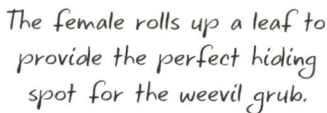

The female rolls up a leaf to provide the perfect hiding spot for the weevil grub.

Location: Mexico, South and Central America, and Caribbean islands

Length: Up to 50 mm (2 in)

The larvae grow under the bark of dead logs and tree trunks, especially on gumbo-limbo trees.

The snout can be longer than the rest of the beetle's body.

Long-snouted weevil

Brentus anchorago

This long, thin weevil might fool predators by looking like a tiny twig! Males use their long snouts to flip each other in tussles over a female. Their small jaws sit at the tip of the snout. Females use these jaws to chew deep holes into dead logs, then lay an egg at the bottom.

Warning signs

Red, orange, and black combinations usually warn predators that the beetle contains toxic chemicals and tastes horrible. Birds and other animals soon learn to avoid these brightly coloured insects.

Bright red with black spots tells predators to stay away.

Bright colours

Some beetles have vibrant colours and beautiful patterns that people love to study. Even tiny beetles often show pretty markings under a hand lens or microscope. These patterns can help them hide, because they break up their body shape. Birds spot insects by their outlines, but patches of colour can confuse them.

Wasp mimics

Black-and-yellow beetles may look a lot like wasps, but they don't have stingers. However, birds and animals don't know that, and may think twice before attacking something that looks like it could give a painful sting.

Bold patterns

Some patterns are made from different coloured scales, arranged like mosaic tiles to form bars, spots, streaks, or chequers. These striking designs make it harder for predators to spot the beetle as it rests on a leaf.

The dead-nettle leaf beetle's metallic colours change with the light and viewing angle.

Shiny shield

The glint and shine of metallic beetles in the sunlight can dazzle predators, giving the insect time to escape. Their glistening colours can also look like drops of water, allowing the insect to hide in plain sight.

Black on purpose

Deep black is a strong warning colour because it stands out against bare soil or green grass and leaves. Oil beetles are jet black, and also produce an oil that causes blisters on the skin. This is why they are commonly called blister beetles.

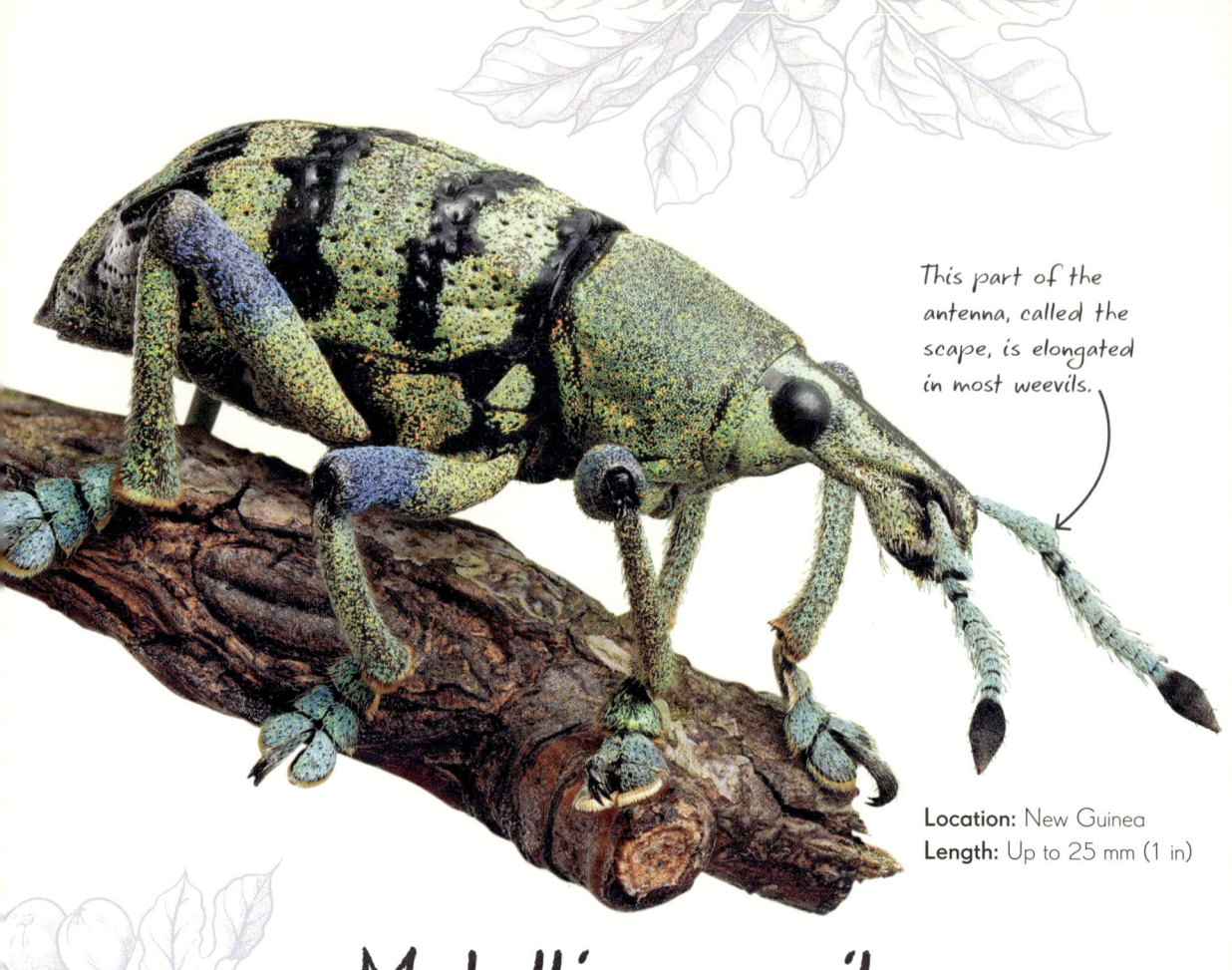

This part of the antenna, called the scape, is elongated in most weevils.

Location: New Guinea
Length: Up to 25 mm (1 in)

Metallic weevil

Eupholus schoenherrii

The metallic weevil looks as if it's been splashed with shiny blue paint, but the colour actually comes from tiny blue scales on its body. These scales don't have any pigment — they're built in a special way that reflects only blue light. Its brilliant spots confuse predators in the dappled light of the forest floor.

Elm bark beetle
Scolytus scolytus

This beetle usually feeds on elm trees. The female bores into the tree trunk and chews a tunnel between the bark and core. She lays an egg, top and bottom, every millimetre or so. The grubs feed on the wood, until they change into adults and chomp their way out of the bark.

Thick clump of hair

Location: Europe, Asia, and Africa
Length: Up to 6 mm (0.2 in)

Grooved wing cases

Tiny hairs for sensing rivals

Location: Colombia and Venezuela
Length: Up to 60 mm (2.4 in)

Rhinoceros beetle

Golofa porteri

The rhinoceros beetle feeds on chusquea bamboo, which is native to South America. Horned males guard their food by sitting head-down on a bamboo stalk. They use the horns on their head and thorax to flip rival beetles into the air. The biggest beetles with the longest horns are usually the winners.

Trilobite beetle
Platerodrilus paradoxus

Female trilobite beetles keep the body shape of the larvae. They have flat, dark bodies with large plates on the front – much like extinct trilobites. Adult females that emerge from the pupae have developed eyes, but no wings.

Location: Southeast Asia
Length: Up to 60 mm (2.4 in)

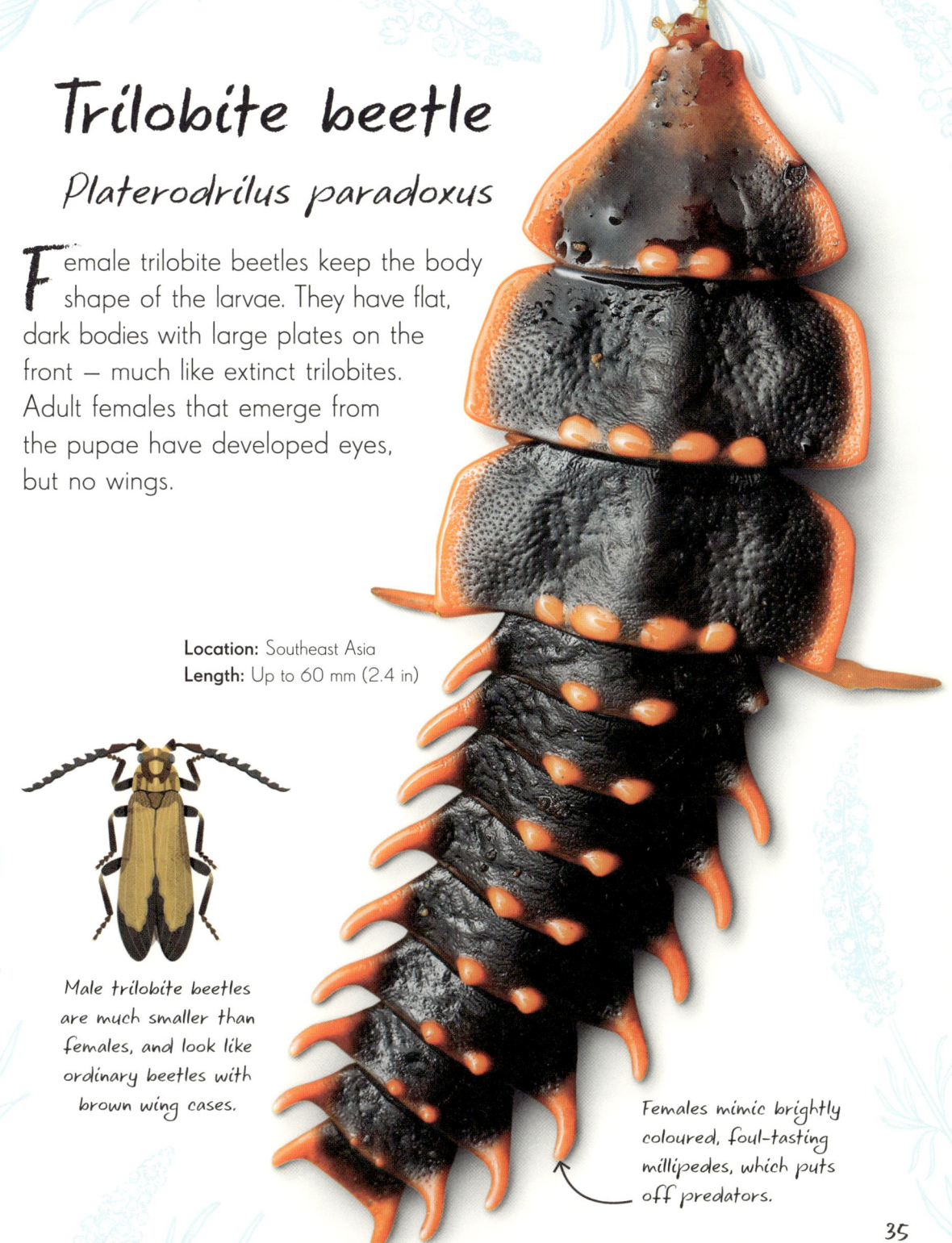

Male trilobite beetles are much smaller than females, and look like ordinary beetles with brown wing cases.

Females mimic brightly coloured, foul-tasting millipedes, which puts off predators.

Conical fungus beetle
Cypherotylus dromedarius

This beetle may confuse enemies with its thorn-like appearance, but that's not part of its defence. Its bold colours warn birds and other animals that it's loaded with foul-tasting chemicals. Predators don't even need to chew it to get the bitter taste. The beetle leaks these chemicals through special pores in its legs and smears them over its body.

The pointed wing cases look like a thorn.

Location: Central and South America
Length: Up to 18 mm (0.7 in)

Location: Central and eastern Asia and Europe
Length: Up to 15 mm (0.6 in)

Feathery antennae

Black-headed cardinal beetle

Pyrochroa coccinea

The black-headed cardinal beetle contains an extremely toxic chemical called cantharidin. Its radiant red colour acts as a strong warning to animals to stay away and not eat it. Cardinal beetles fly readily, and they hold out their brightly coloured wing cases to show off their warning.

Location: Europe and Asia
Length: Up to 12 mm (0.4 in)

The beetle's mottled pattern helps it blend into its surroundings.

It has four yellow-orange bumps on the thorax.

The male's antennae can be up to 60 mm (2.4 in) long.

Timberman
Acanthocinus aedilis

Male timberman beetles have antennae up to five times their body length that trail like streamers as they fly. They probably use them to detect the scent released by females to attract mates. Females also have long antennae, but only about twice their body length. These beetles can survive temperatures as low as −37°C (−35°F).

Scorpion longhorn

Onychocerus albitarsis

This beetle's antennae end in a hook-like thorn. To protect itself, it jabs attackers with its antennae, producing a slight stabbing pain. This isn't just a sharp point, it also contains venom. The scorpion longhorn is the only beetle in the world known to use venom to defend itself.

Location: South America
Length: Up to 21 mm (0.8 in)

Pale blotches on warty body

Smooth, cylindrical thorax

Location: Eastern Brazil
Length: Up to 55 mm (2.2 in)

A ground-dweller, this beetle uses its strong, broad legs to burrow into soil and leaf litter.

Mole beetle

Hypocephalus armatus

Discovered in 1832, this wingless beetle has long puzzled scientists over how it's related to other beetles. Though it has short antennae, the mole beetle is now thought to be part of the longhorn beetle family. For unknown reasons females are much rarer than males.

Caterpillar hunter

Calosoma sycophanta

Although this metallic beetle belongs to the ground beetle group, both adults and larvae can climb trees. They move about in leaves and twigs, where they attack and eat other insects, particularly moth caterpillars. The beetles also take to the air using large wings hidden beneath their wing cases.

This beetle was introduced to North America to help control pest populations of moth caterpillars.

Location: Europe, Asia, and North America
Length: Up to 35 mm (1.4 in)

The metallic colours appear to change at different viewing angles.

Fields and meadows

Filled with flowers and grass, open fields and meadows are the perfect home for a wide variety of beetles. Some live in the root thatch, pushing through tightly packed grass stems and plant roots. Others spend their time munching on all kinds of leaves or visiting flowers to feed on pollen and nectar. In the sunshine, they become livelier, running or flying about swiftly.

The larva digs a vertical tunnel and waits at the entrance with its jaws wide open to trap passing insects, mostly ants.

Pale markings help it blend into the surroundings and stay hidden from predators.

Common claybank tiger beetle
Cicindela limbalis

Location: North America
Length: Up to 16 mm (0.62 in)

True to its name, the claybank tiger beetle hunts much like a tiger. It gives chase to prey before grabbing and crushing it with sharp, powerful jaws. The beetle has very long legs for running fast, and can make rapid, short flights across open bare ground. It is particularly active in hot, dry weather.

Asian bombardier beetle

Pheropsophus jessoensis

This large ground beetle defends itself from predators, especially ants, by squirting hot chemicals from its bottom. Inside its tail tip are two tiny compartments — one holds the chemical hydroquinone, the other hydrogen peroxide. The beetle mixes them in a special chamber, where a chemical reaction heats the mixture to over 100°C (212°F). When threatened, a jet of boiling liquid blasts out.

The beetle has long legs and runs very fast.

Location: China, North and South Korea, and Japan
Length: Up to 20 mm (0.7 in)

The explosion of chemicals makes a loud popping sound.

The beetle's large eyes help it find and kill its prey.

Narrow grass beetle
Ophionea indica

This slim, delicate beetle often wriggles deep into the tightly packed stems of grass tussocks to shelter from cold or rain. Its long legs help it chase down small insects for food. Found in rice fields, this beetle dines on pests like brown planthoppers and rice gall midge flies.

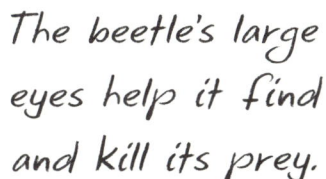

The green and yellow bars on its body help break up its outline as it runs over grass stems.

Location: China, India, and Southeast Asia
Length: Up to 8 mm (0.3 in)

The round body shape helps the beetle push deep into mouldy leaves.

Its dark brown body is covered with pale yellowish hairs.

Location: Europe and East Asia
Length: Up to 0.8 mm (0.03 in)

Featherwing beetle

Acrotrichis montandonii

This beetle is named after its delicate, feather-edged wings. When it flies, it often gets carried by the wind rather than flying in a more controlled manner. The beetle lives in hollow tree trunks or rotting plants, probably feeding on moulds and fungi.

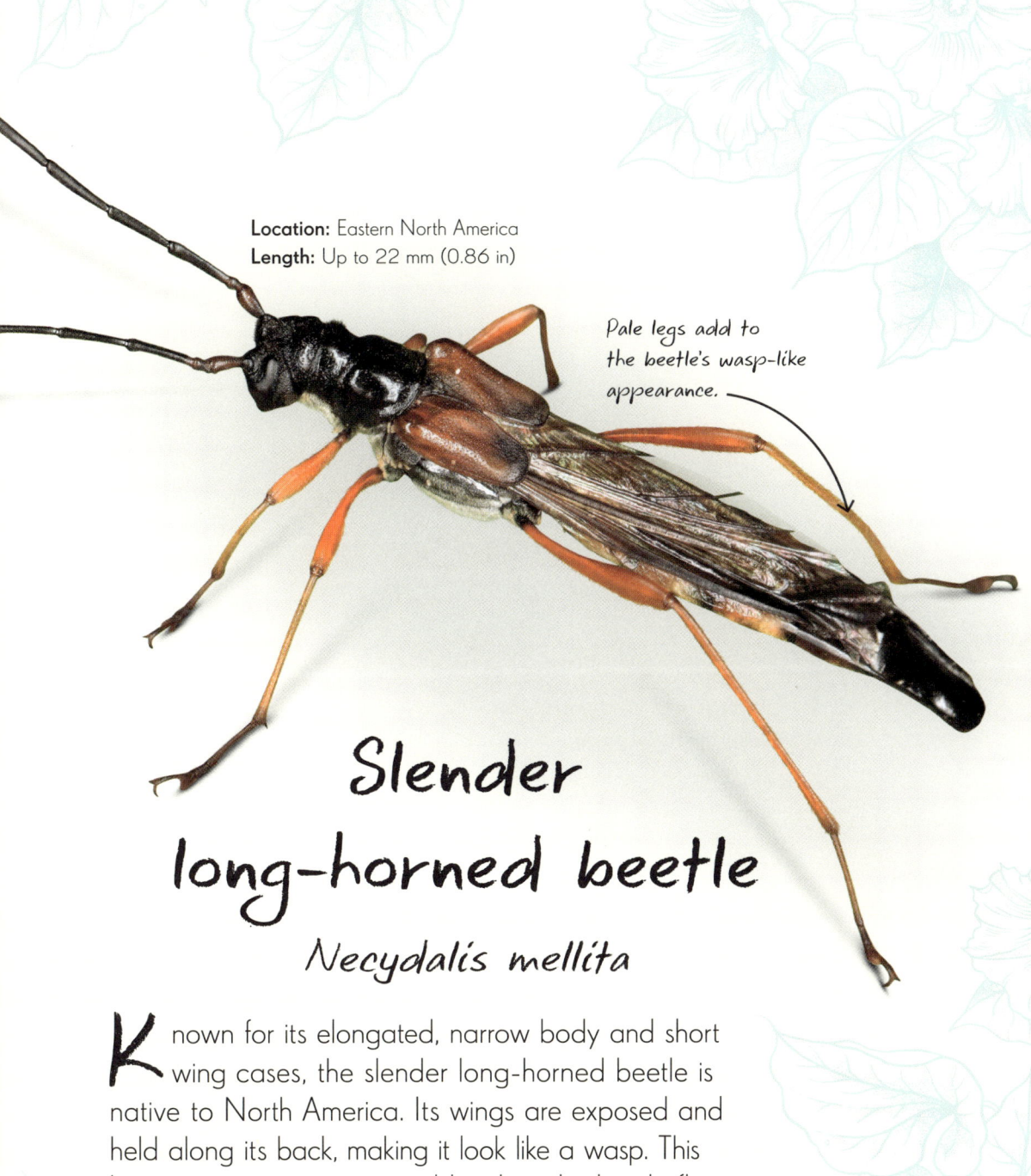

Location: Eastern North America
Length: Up to 22 mm (0.86 in)

Pale legs add to the beetle's wasp-like appearance.

Slender long-horned beetle
Necydalis mellita

Known for its elongated, narrow body and short wing cases, the slender long-horned beetle is native to North America. Its wings are exposed and held along its back, making it look like a wasp. This becomes even more noticeable when the beetle flies from flower to flower.

Dung beetles have short strong legs for digging in the dung and in the soil.

Masters of adaptation

Beetles are full of clever tricks to survive in the wild. Some lay their eggs in animal poo and others live secretly with ants. A few dig through sand, while some squeeze under logs and stones, where other insects cannot reach.

Deep in the dung

The dung tunneller beetle pushes deep into fresh cow or horse droppings to lay its eggs. Its smooth, cylindrical body allows it to move through the muck easily. The grubs then feed on the dung, which still has plenty of nutrients left in it.

Long, thin antennae help the beetle feel its way under the loose tree bark.

Living between layers

The slender body of the flat beetle helps it squeeze under the bark of dead broadleaf and coniferous trees, where it lives. While the larvae feed on decayed bark and fungus in the rotting wood, adults hunt other insects.

Built for sand

The smooth body of the sand ground beetle enables it to push past sand grains without scratching itself. The specialized muscles in its back legs help it to force its way through the loose soil.

The great ant trick

Some ant beetles mimic ant behaviour to stay in ant colonies without being driven away. They produce special chemicals that ants find irresistible and lick off. In return, the beetles are fed by ants or stay safely hidden among them to avoid predators.

A few ant beetles smell like ants to gain easy access to ant nests.

Sacred scarab
Scarabaeus sacer

This beetle rolls a ball of animal dung and buries it in a tunnel, often many metres away. It lays a single egg on the dung and stands guard until the larva begins to feed. The beetle steers the ball by the direction of the sun, going around obstacles but sticking to its course. Long ago, ancient Egyptians linked it to the sun god Khepri, who was thought to roll the sun across the sky.

It stands head-down, pushing the dung ball with its front legs, and uses the long back legs to steer it.

Location: Southern Europe, North Africa, and East Asia
Length: Up to 40 mm (1.6 in)

These super-strong beetles can lift 50 times their own weight.

Males use their head horns to wrestle each other for a meal of sap from a decaying tree.

Location: West Africa
Length: Up to 100 mm (4 in)

Goliath beetle
Goliathus regius

Goliath beetles are among the world's largest and heaviest insects. Despite the size, their strong wings enable them to fly well, with a loud buzzing sound like a small aeroplane. Each beetle has a unique pattern on its back — the left and right sides may not look exactly the same.

Asian longhorn

Anoplophora glabripennis

The larvae of the Asian longhorn chew through the wood of trees, especially poplars and maples, and can even kill healthy ones. Originally from East Asia, they have been accidentally brought to other places, where they've become a serious concern in forests and cities.

Tiny fluffy hairs on the shiny body create a white pattern.

Location: North and South Korea, China, Japan, Europe, and North America
Length: Up to 40 mm (1.6 in)

Location: China, India, and Southeast Asia
Length: Up to 6 mm (0.2 in)

The slim legs do not have any spines.

Rice hispa
Dicladispa armigera

This beetle is covered in long, sharp spines that help protect it from being eaten. Any predator that tries to swallow it is in for a nasty surprise! While adults feed on the upper side of rice leaves, the larvae burrow inside, causing the crop to wilt or die. With each female laying 50–100 eggs in a lifetime, rice hispa is a major rice-field pest.

Location: Europe, Asia, North and South America, North Africa, and Australia
Length: Up to 8 mm (0.3 in)

The pattern on its body is made up of pale hairs.

Thistle weevil

Rhinocyllus conicus

Originally from Europe and Asia, the thistle weevil is now also found in most parts of the world. Each female lays about 100 eggs in flower buds. Once hatched, the larvae munch on the flower heads, reducing the number of thistle seeds produced. Since thistles are weeds, this helps grasses in pastures grow better.

Minotaur beetle

Typhaeus typhoeus

This beetle is named after the Minotaur, a Greek mythical creature with a human body and the head of a bull. Males and females dig burrows up to 1.5 m (5 ft) deep, and carry animal dung inside. Females lay eggs on the dung and the larvae later feed on it. Males fight for control over the tunnel — the one with the biggest horns wins the female and the dung stores.

Location: Europe and North Africa
Length: Up to 24 mm (0.9 in)

Ridges on wing cases

← Nearly transparent rim

Location: North and South America
Length: Up to 7 mm (0.27 in)

Golden tortoise beetle

Charidotella sexpunctata

Tortoise beetles have a flat rim around their body. When threatened, they press down against the leaf surface, pull in their legs and antennae, and sit tight. Nothing can get a grip on them. The males can also change their colour between gold, orange, brown, and purple to distract enemies.

The spiny larva covers itself with its own droppings to hide from predators.

Glow-worm
Lampyris noctiluca

This beetle gets its name from the female, which looks like a worm, without wings or wing cases. At night, she glows in the grass, attracting males to her faint light. This is produced by a chemical reaction in special organs near her tail.

Location: Europe and Asia
Length: Up to 20 mm (0.7 in)

The yellow-green light warns predators not to eat the foul-tasting insect.

Globe scarab beetle
Ceratocanthus aeneus

This strange little beetle rolls up into a near perfect sphere if disturbed, just like a tiny armadillo. The globe scarab beetle tucks its head and thorax down, draws in its antennae, and uses its flat legs to cover its abdomen. It is found in rotten wood and tree holes high above the ground.

The beetle measures 5 mm (0.19 in) across when it curls into a ball.

Shiny, metallic body

Location: Eastern USA
Length: Up to 7 mm (0.27 in)

Only the males have feathery antennae.

Location: Eastern Australia
Length: Up to 19 mm (0.74 in)

Cicada parasite beetle
Rhipicera femorata

Unlike most beetles that have 11 segments in each antenna, the male cicada parasite beetle has more than 20. Its feathery antennae help it find females by detecting the smell of special chemical signals. Adult males and females die shortly after mating and laying eggs. The larvae live in the soil, attacking and feeding on cicada nymphs.

It often chooses bright yellow flowers to feed on pollen.

Location: Europe and Asia
Length: Up to 7 mm (0.27 in)

Golden-green pot beetle

Cryptocephalus sericeus

This shiny beetle looks as if it's made of polished metal. Its body is dotted with tiny dimples. The adults visit flowers for pollen, while the larvae eat dead leaves. The young live inside "pots" — long, rounded cases made from their own poo — with just their head and legs sticking out.

Mushroom rove beetle
Oxyporus rufus

The beetle can most notably be spotted in mushroom gills – plate-like structures on the underside.

Although this rove beetle has large jaws, it is not a predator. Instead, it feeds on fungi, such as mushrooms. Its large flight wings are folded up many times and tucked away under very short wing cases. This allows the beetle flexibility to squeeze into holes in the fungus.

Location: Europe
Length: Up to 10 mm (0.4 in)

Black and orange body

The wing cases are narrowed at the tips, and do not completely cover the flight wings.

Location: Europe and North Africa
Length: Up to 9 mm (0.35 in)

Thick-legged flower beetle

Oedemera nobilis

Only the males have thick, curved back legs. In females, the back legs are long and slender, just like the other four. Nobody knows why this is so, even though the beetle is common and widespread. Males could possibly use them while impressing a mate or fighting each other for territory.

Cockchafer

Melolontha melolontha

This large beetle is known for its loud, buzzing flight. It can usually be spotted between May and June, so is sometimes called Maybug or June bug. As an adult, it lives for just a few weeks, but spends 3–4 years as a larva feeding on plant roots in the ground.

Each antenna of males has seven flat blades, while females have six.

In 1574, a large number of cockchafers fell into the UK's River Severn and clogged the wheels of the water mills.

Location: Europe
Length: Up to 30 mm (1.2 in)

Its body colour can vary from pale yellow to reddish orange.

Location: Central and South America
Length: Up to 24 mm (0.9 in)

Starburst chafer

Gymnetis stellata

No two beetles of this species have exactly the same pattern. The radiating stripes, bars, and rows of spots and speckles vary. Some starburst chafers have dark, bold markings. Others are almost entirely orange with just a few black flecks. These patterns make it hard to spot them on flower heads.

Tufted jewel beetle

Julodis cirrosa

The stiff hairs are longest and thickest on the head and thorax.

This beetle is covered in tufts of stiff hairs coated with a waxy substance. This helps it blend in among thorny bushes. The tough, sticky hairs may also protect it from being eaten, as they can get caught in the beak or mouth of a predator. Adults feed on pollen, while the larvae bore through plant roots.

When females release a special chemical scent, or pheromone, males fly towards them by following the smell.

Location: South Africa
Length: Up to 37 mm (1.4 in)

Willow flea beetle
Crepidodera aurata

This brilliantly shiny beetle has large, muscular legs. When threatened, it tenses its muscles, then suddenly releases them — springing high into the air like a flea. This is how the beetle gets its name. The willow flea beetle can jump more than 60 cm (24 in), which is nearly 250 times its own body length.

Pale antennae darken towards the tips.

Location: Europe and Asia
Length: Up to 2.5 mm (0.09 in)

Wing cases have a metallic sheen.

Their larvae graze the surface of leaves, forming small windows.

Location: Europe
Length: Up to 18 mm (0.7 in)

Long legs help it run quickly to escape danger.

Snail-killer beetle

Cychrus caraboides

The snail-killer beetle lives in moss and leaf litter in damp woodlands. It mainly feeds on snails found there. The beetle uses its narrow head and thorax to reach deep into the snail shells. It makes a loud squeaking sound by rubbing its wings against a row of ridges on the abdomen. It does this perhaps to communicate or warn off danger.

Parks and gardens

You can find beetles everywhere — from the local public park to your own garden, or on road verges and along hedgerows. They visit flowers, rest on leaves and stems, climb tree trunks, or hide under logs and stones. They also run around on the ground, often in bright sunshine. While some beetles might damage flowers and plants, others help protect them. They go after mealybugs and other harmful insects, and are often considered a gardener's friend.

It has three spots on each wing case and one across the joint near its thorax.

It squeezes foul-tasting blood through its leg joints to deter enemies like birds.

Seven-spot ladybird

Coccinella septempunctata

Location: Europe, Africa, and eastern Asia
Length: Up to 7 mm (0.27 in)

This magnificent beetle is named after the Virgin Mary, the mother of Jesus, who was often shown in a red cloak in paintings. Ladybirds are welcomed in gardens as they feed on aphids — a common pest. Their bold colours and patterns warn enemies not to eat them as they're packed with poisons and taste horrid.

The parts between the net-like ridges on the wing cases are thin and see-through.

The larvae feed in the rotten wood of logs and stumps.

Location: West Australia, Tasmania, and New Zealand
Length: Up to 15 mm (0.6 in)

Net-winged beetle

Distocupes varians

The net-like pattern on its wing cases is similar to the lacy wings of lacewings — a closely related insect group. Experts believe this pattern may relate to how early beetle ancestors looked before modern beetles began evolving 300–350 million years ago.

Great diving beetle

Dytiscus marginalis

Diving beetles can breathe underwater by carrying a thin bubble of air down with them, underneath their tight-fitting wing cases. When they need more air, they rise to the surface and stick just the tip of their tail out of water.

Its back legs, fringed with hairs, work like oars to help it swim quickly.

Location: Europe and Asia
Length: Up to 35 mm (1.37 in)

Unlike females that have wrinkled wing cases, males have smooth ones.

Location: Western half of North America
Length: Up to 30 mm (1.2 in)

Ten-lined June beetle
Polyphylla decimlineata

The June beetle is found in areas with sandy soil. It is named so because it flies actively in June. However, despite its name, the beetle has only eight and two half white lines, instead of 10. Although a large-sized beetle, it flies well, often attracted to street lamps or lit windows. The larvae feed on plant roots, while adults nibble on pine needles and other tree leaves.

The yellow dusting and white lines are made of coloured scales and hairs.

Location: Europe and Asia
Length: Up to 24 mm (0.9 in)

Rose chafer

Cetonia aurata

Most beetles fly with their wing cases held open, but rose chafers fly with theirs only partially open. A special curved notch near the base allows it to open its wing cases, extend the broad flight wings, and then close the cases down again. This enables the wings to flap freely. Very few beetles can do this.

The adults visit flowers to feed on pollen and petals.

The adults are active in May, when they fly about searching for flowers.

Bee chafer
Trichius fasciatus

The adult beetles visit flowers to eat pollen and nibble on petals, and when they fly, they look just like bumblebees. With black and orange bars, and long yellowish hairs covering their thorax and abdomen, the resemblance is striking. The chafers often live in cool places, further north, and higher up in the mountains, similar to bumblebees.

The black marks on the orange wing cases vary in size between beetles.

Location: Europe and northern Asia
Length: Up to 12 mm (0.4 in)

The beetle's entire body, including its underside, is brightly coloured.

Location: India and Southeast Asia
Length: Up to 48 mm (1.8 in)

Jewel beetle
Sternocera aequisignata

This metallic green beetle really lives up to its name — it looks just like a living jewel. In fact, jewel beetle wing cases have been made into jewellery for centuries. Its dazzling colour comes from tiny, microscopic grooves on its wing cases that reflect light in a similar way as polished metal.

One with the bark

Many beetles are covered with tiny coloured scales and hairs, arranged in different patterns. These markings make them look like tree bark, bare soil, or dead leaves in their natural habitats.

A long-horned beetle on the surface of a tree

The mottled pattern of the pine weevil is a perfect match for the bark of pine trees.

Camouflage

One of the best ways for a beetle to avoid being eaten is to blend, or camouflage, itself into its surroundings. Sometimes this means being green like the leaf it rests on. Other times, it may be patterned in browns, greys, or yellows to match the colours of soil, tree bark, or dead leaves.

Rounded, flat body

Bump on a leaf

Some green tortoise beetles have no markings. When they pull in their legs and antennae under their thorax and wing cases, they look like small bumps on a leaf surface and often go unnoticed.

Hidden in the riverbed

This bright water beetle has vivid patterns on its body. But instead of making it stand out, the spots help it blend in. The insect stays hidden when sitting on the sandy bottom of shallow streams.

The sunburst diving beetle breathes underwater with the help of air stored in a water bubble under its wing cases.

Vanishing in the sand

The pine chafer is a large beetle. However, its dark body is covered in pale markings, which allow it to almost disappear when crawling over sandy ground.

Its wing cases can be brown, black, or reddish-brown.

This North American beetle is also called the Big Dipper firefly for its curved, dipping light flash.

Common eastern firefly

Photinus pyralis

As the beetle flies, it gives off a single long flash of light and performs a series of vertical loops. The light traces the bottom of the loop and continues into the upswing, creating a unique light signal shaped like the letter J. Each flash lasts more than about 0.3 seconds. If a female responds with a flash, usually 1–2 seconds later, the male flies towards her to mate.

Location: Eastern North America
Length: Up to 15 mm (0.6 in)

Light is emitted from an organ on the underside of its tail.

Location: Worldwide, except the Poles
Length: Up to 3 mm (0.1 in)

The round wing cases cover almost the entire abdomen.

Smooth spider beetle
Gibbium aequinoctiale

This small beetle has hitched a ride around the world with humans, hiding in stored goods. It couldn't have travelled on its own because it has no wings and cannot fly. The beetle eats just about anything — spilled food, animal droppings, nest material, leather, and wool. Found almost throughout the world, it usually lives in buildings and warehouses.

Horned fungus beetle
Bolitotherus cornutus

Only males of this species have the long, curved horns on their thorax to use in push-and-shove contests. The biggest male with the largest horns usually wins — claiming both the female and the prized birch polypore fungus, which is where the females lay their eggs.

Its body is lined with bumps and warts.

Location: North America
Length: Up to 13 mm (0.5 in)

Death-watch beetle
Xestobium rufovillosum

This large woodworm beetle lives in tree trunks, especially oak, and in old wooden beams and rafters. The male bangs his head rapidly on the wood to send a loud ticking signal — and the female ticks back. They keep calling until they find each other in the deep dark tunnels hollowed out in the timber. In the past, its mating call was thought to predict an approaching death!

Location: Europe, Asia, and North America
Length: Up to 8 mm (0.3 in)

Light-coloured hairs stand out against its brown body.

Location: Central Europe
Length: Up to 45 mm (1.7 in)

When disturbed, it ejects a toxic, oily chemical from its leg joints to defend itself.

It has 11 segments in its antennae.

Speckled oil beetle
Meloe variegatus

The female lays thousands of tiny eggs at a time and is often referred to as a "walking bag of eggs". The eggs hatch into long-legged larvae called triungulins. The juveniles climb up flowers and grab onto passing insects, but only a lucky few manage to ride on the solitary bee to its nest. There, they feast on bee grubs and stored pollen or nectar.

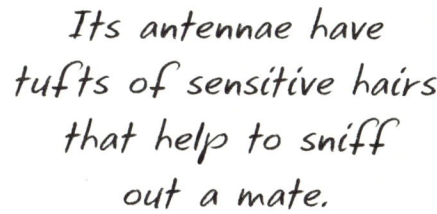

Its antennae have tufts of sensitive hairs that help to sniff out a mate.

Location: Central and southern Europe
Length: Up to 40 mm (1.6 in)

Alpine longhorn
Rosalia alpina

This beetle lives only in the beech forests of Europe. Its cream-coloured larvae spend about 3 years munching through decayed beech tree trunks and stumps. The adult's black markings vary — no two individuals have exactly the same pattern. They help break up the outline of the beetle when it is resting on a tree trunk, making it harder to spot.

Most parts of its body are covered with dusty blue hairs.

83

Location: Southern China, Southeast Asia, Indonesia, and Australia
Length: Up to 10 mm (0.39 in)

Broad, flat feet help the beetle grip smooth leaves.

The female coats each egg with her poo to hide it from predators.

Coconut hispine
Brontispa longissima

The larvae of this beetle feed on coconut palm leaves and can cause serious damage to plantations. The adult beetle is narrow and flat, perfect for slipping between tightly packed leaves to hide along the tree trunk. Originally from Indonesia, it now lives in coconut trees in a few other countries as well.

Location: North America, Europe, and Asia
Length: Up to 11 mm (0.4 in)

Each wing case has five yellow and five black stripes.

Colorado potato beetle
Leptinotarsa decemlineata

First discovered over 200 years ago, this beetle fed on a wild plant called buffalo burr in the Rocky Mountains, USA. As farmers began to grow potatoes in the beetle's range, it started feeding on them and spread across North America. It was accidentally brought to France around 1920 and is now a widespread potato pest across Europe.

A single female can lay up to 500 bright orange eggs, packed in clusters beneath leaves.

Bloody-nosed beetle
Timarcha tenebricosa

Location: Europe
Length: Up to 18 mm (0.7 in)

Black is a strong warning colour, telling predators to back off as the beetle is packed with foul-tasting chemicals. If picked up, it gives a nasty taste of the toxins by squeezing bright red blood out through special holes near its mouth. This looks as if the beetle has a nose bleed — a defence mechanism called reflex bleeding.

Bright red blob of blood is released here.

Palm weevil
Rhynchophorus ferrugineus

This weevil's large grubs, called sago worms, bore tunnels up to 1 m (3 ft) long in palm tree trunks. Originally from southern Asia, it was accidentally introduced to Mediterranean Europe about 40 years ago. There, it attacks ornamental trees in towns and cities, causing them to wilt and die, leaving gaps in carefully landscaped streets.

Location: Southeast Asia, Mediterranean region, Arabian Peninsula, and India
Length: Up to 40 mm (1.6 in)

The wing cases are strongly and deeply grooved.

Acorn weevil
Curculio glandium

This weevil is known for its extra-long snout, with powerful jaws at the tip. The female uses hers to drill a deep hole into an acorn and lays an egg inside. Later, the grub eats the nutritious centre of the acorn. When the fruit falls in autumn, the juvenile chews its way out and makes its pupa in the soil to change into an adult.

Location: Europe
Length: Up to 6 mm (0.2 in)

The snout is about the same length as the body.

Location: Europe
Length: Up to 7 mm (0.27 in)

Its smooth, shiny body glints in the sun, confusing predators just long enough to escape.

Whirligig beetle

Gyrinus substriatus

Whirligigs get their name from their erratic spins across the surface of ponds and lakes. This makes it difficult for predators to catch them. Each of their eyes is split in two — one half watches the sky above for danger, the other scans the water below for prey.

The split eyes are positioned vertically on each side of its head.

Devil's coach-horse

Ocypus olens

This large insect belongs to the rove beetle family, which has very short wing cases and exposed abdomens. It has fully functional flight wings that are folded tightly underneath its short wing cases. However, this beetle rarely flies and prefers to run fast. It attacks and kills small insects for food, as well as worms, spiders, and carrion.

To scare off attackers, it raises its tail and releases a smelly droplet.

Location: Europe and North America
Length: Up to 32 mm (1.25 in)

The wing cases are broad and the veins form ridges along them.

The beetle opens its wing cases when threatened.

Location: Eastern North America and Mexico
Length: Up to 18 mm (0.7 in)

Banded net-winged beetle
Calopteron reticulatum

This brightly coloured beetle is in no hurry to flee from predators. It moves slowly and when it flies, it flutters gently like a small moth. It is packed with poisonous chemicals that taste horrible if anything tries to eat it. The larvae feed on rotting wood, while adults likely just sip nectar from flowers.

Mealybug destroyer was one of the first predatory insects purposely released to target a pest.

Dark brown, domed beetle with an orange head and tail.

Mealybug destroyer

Cryptolaemus montrouzieri

Location: Australia, Europe, Asia, North Africa, and North and South America
Length: Up to 4.5 mm (0.1 in)

Near the end of the 19th century, citrus mealybugs had become a major pest on orange trees in California, USA. Covered in white, waxy hair, they looked unappetizing, and none of the American predators would eat them. This Australian beetle was deliberately released into the orange groves to consume the mealybugs.

Tumbling flower beetle

Mordella leucosticta

These beetles are often found buzzing from flower to flower, feeding on pollen. When disturbed, they flick their long back legs to skip and jump. This rapidly rotates their body left and right around the long pointed tail, until they drop to the ground.

Pale spots help the beetle blend in as it rests on a flower.

Location: Australia
Length: Up to 10 mm (0.39 in)

Musk beetle

Aromia moschata

This beetle gets its interesting name from the musky smell produced by special glands on its thorax. One of the chemicals released is rose oxide, which is also used in perfumes. The strong scent is thought to help put off predators.

Location: Europe and northern Asia
Length: Up to 35 mm (1.37 in)

The larvae chew deep tunnels in willow, poplar, or alder trees.

Very long antennae

Location: Europe, Asia, and North Africa
Length: Up to 30 mm (1.2 in)

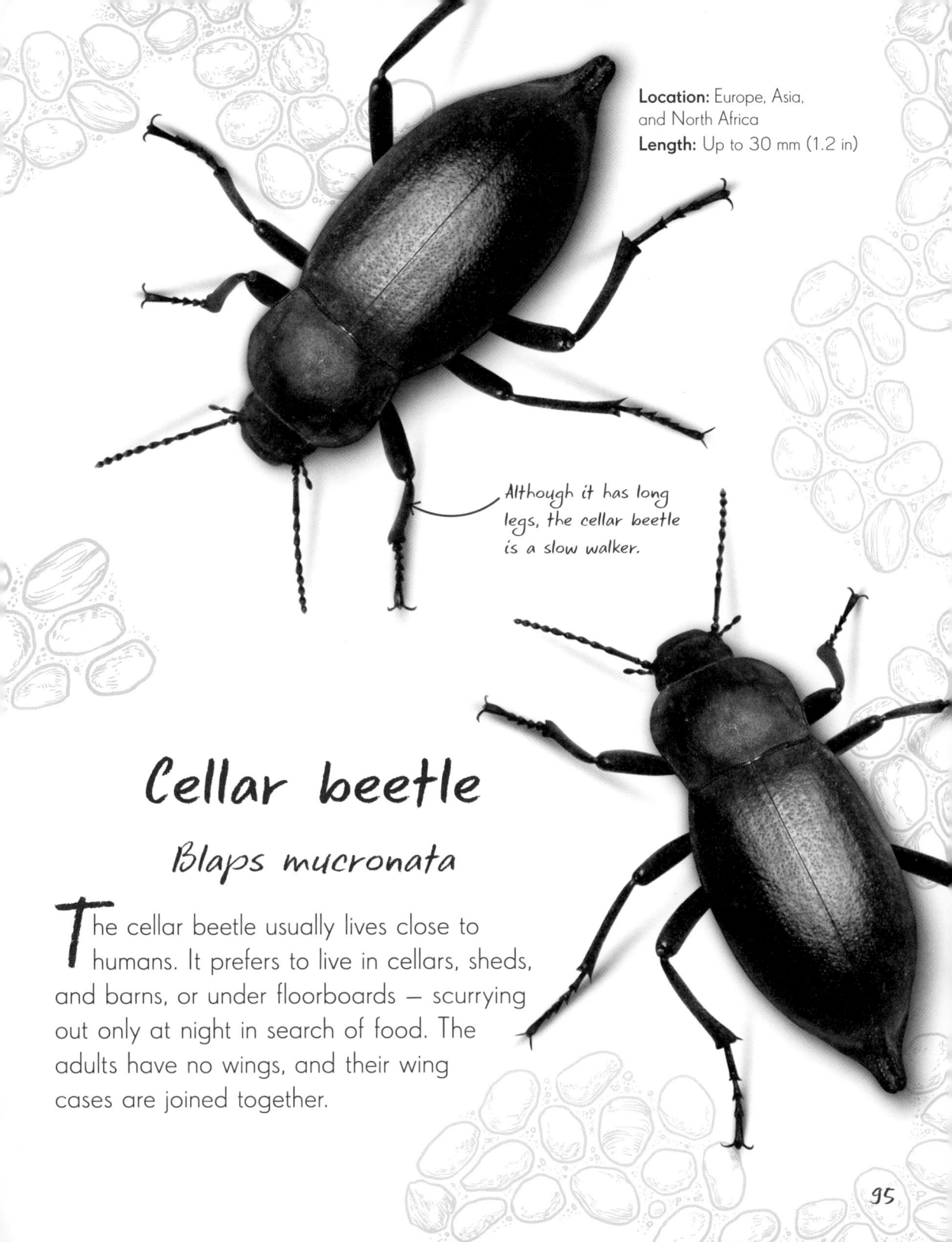

Although it has long legs, the cellar beetle is a slow walker.

Cellar beetle

Blaps mucronata

The cellar beetle usually lives close to humans. It prefers to live in cellars, sheds, and barns, or under floorboards — scurrying out only at night in search of food. The adults have no wings, and their wing cases are joined together.

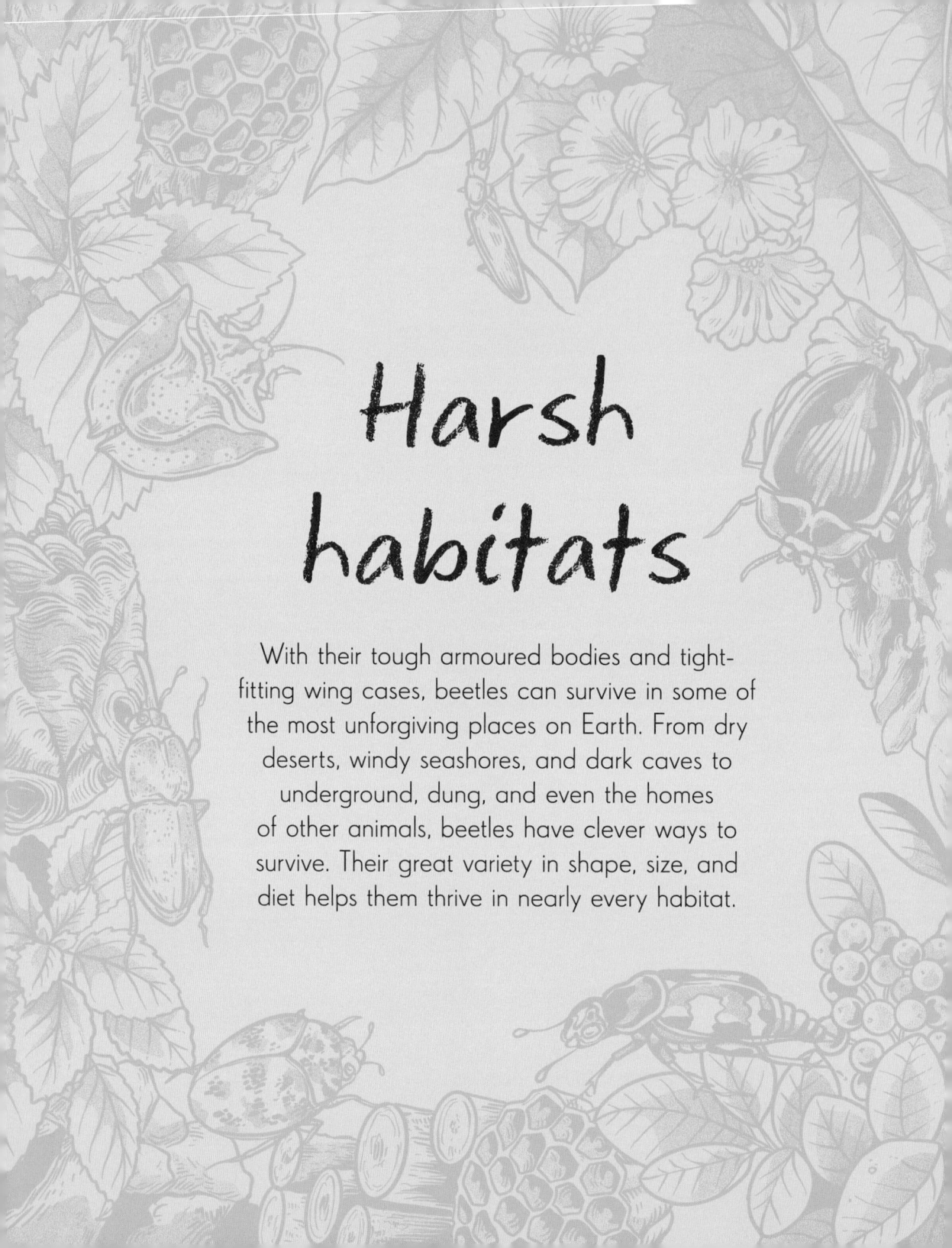

Harsh habitats

With their tough armoured bodies and tight-fitting wing cases, beetles can survive in some of the most unforgiving places on Earth. From dry deserts, windy seashores, and dark caves to underground, dung, and even the homes of other animals, beetles have clever ways to survive. Their great variety in shape, size, and diet helps them thrive in nearly every habitat.

Manticore beetle
Manticora latipennis

Also called monster tiger beetle, this is the largest member of the tiger beetle family. It lives in the dry, sandy areas of southern Africa. Using its long legs, the beetle easily chases down caterpillars, grasshoppers, and other prey. It then grabs its victim with its large, powerful jaws for a hearty meal.

The male beetle is especially known for its uneven, sickle-shaped jaws.

Strong jaws hold the prey in place as the beetle devours it.

Location: Southwest Africa
Length: Up to 60 mm (2.4 in)

Sand beetle
Omophron limbatum

This ground beetle is shaped like a water beetle, but does not swim. Instead, its smooth, teardrop body lets it push itself easily into the moist sand on riverbanks and pond edges. It hides in its burrow by day and comes out at night to chase down and feed on small insects.

Mottled markings on its back help it blend in with the sand grains.

Location: Europe, North Africa, and Asia
Length: Up to 7 mm (0.27 in)

Location: Worldwide, except Antarctica
Length: Up to 9 mm (0.35 in)

Thanks to refrigerators, this beetle is a less common food pest today.

Pale band of hairs across the body

Bacon beetle

Dermestes lardarius

In the wild, this beetle feeds on carrion when little is left but bones, sinew, fur, and feathers. It also thrives in human homes, feeding on stored meat products like bacon, animal fats like cheese, dried fish, leather, and furs. The bacon beetle was accidentally spread by humans and is now found across the world.

Himalayan burying beetle

Nicrophorus nepalensis

Also called the "undertaker beetle", the male and female work together to sniff out dead animals, such as rats and birds. Then, they dig out soil from beneath the corpse until it settles into the hole. The excavated soil falls over to cover the carcass, which is rolled into a ball. The female lays eggs in a dip on top of this corpse ball.

Mainly black antennae with orange tips

Location: Central, east, and Southeast Asia
Length: Up to 30 mm (1.2 in)

It has shorter legs than its cousins, the long-legged ground beetles.

Location: Congo, Kenya, Malawi, South Africa, and Tanzania
Length: Up to 27 mm (1.06 in)

Detailed, ornate antennae

Ant nest beetle

Cerapterus pilipennis

This clever beetle lives its entire life among ants in their nests. It releases a chemical from its antennae that ants eagerly lick up, treating it as a fellow ant mate. The chemical mimics the substance that ants release to communicate with each other in the nest.

Cave beetle

Leptodirus hochenwartii

This rare beetle lives in the dark caves. With nothing to see and nowhere to go, the cave beetle has no eyes or wings. It lays eggs that hatch into fully-grown larvae that do not eat. The juveniles immediately pupate and change into adults.

Long antennae help it find its way in complete darkness.

Location: Eastern Italy, Croatia, and Slovenia
Length: Up to 11 mm (0.4 in)

House longhorn
Hylotrupes bajulus

This longhorn beetle sometimes feeds in old pine trees in the wild, but can severely damage joist timbers and wooden rafters in the roofs of houses. Its larvae bore large holes in the wood, often weakening it to the point of collapse. The house longhorn thrives in the timber used in construction.

The black body is covered with tiny pale hairs.

Location: Worldwide, except Antarctica
Length: Up to 27 mm (1.06 in)

Metallic violet or purple in colour

Location: Western coasts of North Africa and Europe
Length: Up to 4 mm (0.15 in)

Short antennae end in small, club-like structures.

Sea lavender weevil

Pseudaplemonus limonii

This attractive weevil lives in coastal salt marshes, feeding on sea lavender. At low tide, it crawls over leaves and flowers. But when the tide comes in, it pushes down into tight leaf bases or the mud around stalks and roots for refuge. This helps the beetle survive when completely submerged in salt water.

Northern dune tiger beetle
Cicindella hybrida

Sand dunes are difficult habitats for insects. Dry and exposed, with little plant shelter, the desert constantly changes as the wind whips at the loose sand grains. However, the dune tiger beetle thrives here. It attacks and eats the other small insects struggling in harsh landscape. Running fast on its long legs, it makes short flying jumps to catch prey in the air.

Location: Europe, North Africa, and Asia
Length: Up to 16 mm (0.62 in)

The beetle's colours help camouflage it against the sandy soil.

Location: Southern and eastern Africa
Length: Up to 13 mm (0.5 in)

The beetle is entirely red, except for its black legs and antennae.

Poison arrow beetle

Diamphidia femoralis

This small leaf beetle is found only in southern Africa. Its larvae feed on toxic commiphora plants. After a hearty meal, they smear their bodies with their own poo to avoid being eaten by predators. In southern Africa, the San people coat their arrow tips with the beetles' pupae, which are toxic enough to kill a large giraffe.

Drugstore beetle
Stegobium paniceum

This beetle was once commonly found in pharmacies, hiding in pill bottles and eating the plant material used to make pills. That's how it got its name. Today, the beetle infests, or attacks, a wide variety of dried foods – from biscuits and breads to the hottest chilli powder.

Location: Worldwide, except Antarctica
Length: Up to 3.5 mm (0.13 in)

Reddish-brown with rows of small pits on wing cases

The beetle also feeds on biscuits and gets extra nutrients through moulds like yeast growing in the chewings.

Bumblebee rove beetle

Emus hirtus

This beetle actively flies about on fresh cow dung. It uses its fiercely sharp jaws to catch and eat the flies which are also attracted to the dung. In flight, the rove beetle looks like a bumblebee. It is called the "Maid of Kent" in England because it's only found around the Isle of Sheppey, in north Kent.

Despite being so hairy, sticky cow dung does not cling to its body.

Location: Europe and West Asia
Length: Up to 26 mm (1.02 in)

Its body is entirely covered in dense, short hairs.

Bee beetle
Trichodes apiarius

This brightly coloured beetle visits flowers to eat pollen, but it will also occasionally eat other small insects. The bee beetle lays its eggs in the soil, inside burrow nests made by small bees. The larvae then feed on the bees' stored food and bee grubs.

Early larvae are pink or yellow in colour, with flattened, hairy bodies.

Location: Europe, North Africa, and West Asia
Length: Up to 15 mm (0.6 in)

Wasp nest beetle
Metoecus paradoxus

This beetle lays its eggs on old tree trunks and logs. The tiny larvae, called triungulins, climb onto the bodies of common wasps that visit the wood to chew it and make paper for their nests. Unknowingly, the wasps carry the larvae home, where they feast on wasp grubs. The juveniles pupate there, emerging as adults the following year when the wasps are starting to build their new nests.

It is also called eyelash beetle because its antennae look like false eyelashes.

Orange wing cases with black tips

Long, feathery antennae

Location: Europe
Length: Up to 12 mm (0.4 in)

Black bumps on pale body

Location: Central and South America
Length: Up to 45 mm (1.7 in)

Ironclad beetle
Zopherus chilensis

Short, segmented antennae

This beetle gets its name from its extra-hard body, which seems as if it's covered in iron. It lives in dry forests, where both adults and larvae feed on fungi growing on dead trees. Slow-moving and wingless, the beetle often plays dead when disturbed.

Pie-dish beetle
Helea tuberculata

This strange-looking beetle comes with its own built-in shield — a broad ledge around its body. This allows the beetle to avoid small predators like ants because when it clamps down, they can't grab its legs. The ledge also works like a rain gutter, collecting moisture for the insect to drink.

Location: Southwest Australia
Length: Up to 20 mm (0.7 in)

Dark body colour

Wharf borer larvae are usually off-white or creamy white in colour.

Long antennae are about half its body length.

Location: Worldwide, except Antarctica
Length: Up to 15 mm (0.6 in)

Wharf borer
Nacerdes melanura

The larvae of the wharf borer tunnel into the wooden timbers of boats, piers, jetties, and quays. They feed deep inside the wood and are usually covered by water at high tide. They once caused serious damage, when most harbour structures were made of wood instead of concrete or iron.

Grain weevil
Sitophilus granarius

It is thought that this beetle originated in North Africa, but it is now found worldwide. The grain weevil lives only in grain stores and is a major pest of stored wheat. The female uses her jaws to chew a deep hole into a wheat grain, then turns around to lay an egg inside. The grub hatches, eats the grain hollow, and later emerges to change into an adult.

The beetle's colour can vary from dark brown to black.

The beetle's small jaws are right at the end of its long snout.

Location: Worldwide, except Antarctica
Length: Up to 3.5 mm (0.13 in)

Green-footed peacock beetle

Elaphrus riparius

This small beetle runs about on the damp edges of ponds and streams. The irregular patterns on its body help it blend in with the waterside plants. The mirror-like areas glint in the sunshine, mixing in with the reflections from the wet mud. It hunts other tiny insects, especially springtails. The beetle's large eyes help it find prey and spot any predators.

Dull green patterns and shiny spots confuse predators.

Location: Europe, Asia, and North Africa
Length: Up to 8 mm (0.3 in)

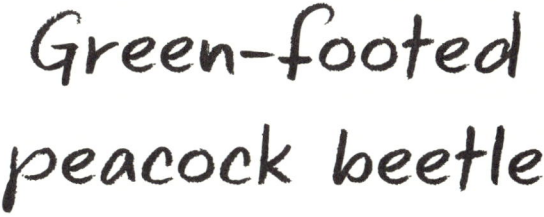

Location: North America, Europe, North Africa, and Asia
Length: Up to 12 mm (0.4 in)

The beetle's colour blends in with the soot-blackened wood of a burned log.

Black fire beetle

Melanophila acuminata

This beetle lays its eggs in freshly burned conifer logs. Special sensors under its thorax detect infrared light from fires up to 130 km (81 miles) away. Living pine trees are full of sticky sap, which puts off many wood-boring beetles like this one. But, since burned trees have none of this syrupy liquid, black fire beetles thrive in them.

Red flour beetle
Tribolium castaneum

True to its name, the red flour beetle can be commonly found in stored flour and other dried foods. It's considered a troublesome pest in mills, granaries, and warehouses across the world. Since it's quick to rear, the beetle is widely used in laboratories to study insect behaviour and growth.

Its larvae feed in the ground seeds of wheat and other grasses.

Location: Worldwide, except Antarctica
Length: Up to 5 mm (0.19 in)

Smooth and cylindrical body allows it to easily push through the stored flour.

Fighting tortoise beetle
Acromis sparsa

The males of this species have a unique fighting style to win a female. They grab each other between their pointy wing cases and thorax corners, like a pair of pincers. The winner flips the rival off the plant, claiming both the female and the plant. Some males have holes in their wing cases, which are scars from intense fights in the past.

Flattened, transparent wing cases blend into the plant it rests on.

Location: Central and South America
Length: Up to 14 mm (0.5 in)

Distinctive long back legs

Location: Europe and northeast Asia
Length: Up to 11 mm (0.4 in)

Reed beetle

Donacia crassipes

On warm, sunny days, the reed beetles run and fly about on water lily pads in ponds. Adults nibble on the leaves of aquatic plants, keeping to the upper surface. But the larvae feed in plant stems underwater and breathe air passing down hollow tubes inside the plant, using a special breathing spine in their tail.

Fog-basking beetle
Onymacris unguicularis

Location: Namibia
Length: Up to 24 mm (1.02 in)

This beetle lives in one of the driest places on Earth — the Namib Desert in Africa. Rain is rare, but fog drifts in from the Atlantic Ocean. On a sand dune, the beetle tilts its head down and tail up. Ridges on its back trap moisture in the fog and water droplets run down to its mouth — just enough for it to survive.

Long legs allow it to stick its tail up into the air.

Museum beetle
Anthrenus verbasci

The museum beetle has a taste for all sorts. Out in the wild, it feeds on pollen and dead animals when only fur, feathers, and bones remain. In houses, it nibbles on animal fibres like silk and wool, but especially loves feasting on skins, furs, and pinned insect specimens in museums. This is how it gets its unique name.

Location: Worldwide
Length: Up to 3.5 mm (0.13 in)

Overlapping scales create a mottled appearance.

Its larva is commonly called a woolly bear due to the dense, bristly hair on its body.

American burying beetle

Helm's stag beetle

Under protection

Some rare beetles, like the Helm's stag beetle from New Zealand, have been protected by law for a long time. Another species, called the American burying beetle, is critically endangered in the USA, due to habitat loss and overuse of pesticides.

Conservation

Beetles play a crucial role in every habitat they live in. By monitoring their behaviour and numbers, scientists can keep a check on the quality and health of a particular environment. Special measures are also being taken to ensure the population of rare beetles is maintained and does not decline further.

Dead or alive?

For over 100 years, the world's largest water beetle — the Brazilian diving beetle — was known only from a pinned specimen in London. But in 2019, ten more specimens were found at a museum in Paris. However, it remains unknown whether the beetle still survives in the wild.

Environmental clues

Many beetles only feed on a single plant or live in a very specific habitat. By tracking their numbers, scientists can tell if the environment is being damaged, polluted, or destroyed.

Parallelomorphus laevigatus has been used to monitor metal pollution in the food chain of Sicilian beaches in Italy.

A collection of pinned beetles and other insects

Permanent record

Museum specimens are a vital record of beetle diversity — the many shapes, sizes, and colours they come in and the different places they inhabit. Modern studies can be compared with this valuable history.

Glossary

antenna
A long, thin sense organ attached to the head of an insect, containing smell and touch sensors

camouflage
Ability of an animal to blend into its natural surroundings with the help of its colours or patterns

carrion
Dead body of an animal – an important food for many beetle recyclers

dung
Solid droppings of animals. Also called poo

endangered
Any species of animal or plant that is in danger of dying out

exoskeleton
The hard outer shell of a beetle and other animals, which is tough but flexible

fog
Dense cloud of water droplets near the Earth's surface

fruiting body
Spore-making part of a fungus that usually grows above ground

gill
Thin, flattened, spore-bearing structures on the underside of mushroom caps and sometimes also on the stem of fruit bodies

habitat
Natural home of an animal

infrared
Type of warm light that can't be seen by humans

joist
Long piece of timber or steel that supports a building

juvenile
Young animal that is not yet fully grown

juvenile hormone
Chemical produced in a larva that stops adult features, such as wings and antennae, from growing until it is fully grown

larva
Young stage of a beetle and other insects that must feed and grow before turning into an adult

leaf litter
Layer of dead and decaying leaves covering the soil underneath living plants

metamorphosis
Process in which an animal changes its shape as it grows into an adult. For example, when a caterpillar changes into a butterfly

microscopic
Something so small that it can only be seen through a microscope

mosaic
Pattern made up of small pieces. In some beetles, scales or hairs of varying sizes and shapes form mosaic-like patterns

mottled
Spotted or patchy colouring

nectar
Sweet, sugary liquid made by flowers to attract insects

nutrient
Chemical in food that helps an animal or plant to live and grow

parasite
Organism that lives on another, getting its food, and usually shelter too, from its victim

pest
Animal that attacks or destroys things, such as crops

pheromone
Special chemical signal given off by an animal to communicate with another

pigment
Coloured chemical or mineral substance

pollination
Movement of pollen, often by insects, from the male part of the plant to the female part of the plant to ensure seed or fruit growth

predator
An animal that catches, kills, and eats other animals

prey
An animal that is hunted and killed by another animal for food

pupa
An insect at the third stage of complete metamorphosis — between larva and adult

refuge
Safe haven or shelter

scale
Tiny, broad, flat structures that cover beetle wing cases, and which give them the variety of different colours and patterns

segment
Single part of a structure that has repeated units, such as on an antenna, leg, or body

sinew
Tough tissue joining muscle to bone

snout
Long extension on the front of the head, with the jaws at the tip

species
Particular type of animal, plant, or other living thing

specimen
Single example of a particular species or type

thorax
Middle segment of an insect, between head and abdomen, that has wings and legs attached

tide
Rising and falling levels of the sea

trilobite
marine animal that existed during the Paleozoic Era

triungulin
Tiny active larva of some beetles that runs about and grabs onto other insects in the hope that it gets taken to the right sort of bee or wasp nest

yeast
Microscopic fungus

Index

A
acorn weevil 88
alpine longhorn 83
American burying beetle 122
ant beetles 49
ant nest beetle 101
antennae 6, 38, 39, 48, 59, 63
ants 43, 44, 48, 49, 101
aphids 69
Asian bombardier beetle 44
Asian longhorn 52

B
bacon beetle 99
banded net-winged beetle 91
bark 14, 19, 20, 27, 29, 33, 48, 76
beautiful carrion beetle 21
bee beetle 109
bee chafer 74
bess beetle 22
Big Dipper 78
bioluminescence 24, 57, 78
black fire beetle 116
black-headed cardinal beetle 37
blood 69, 86
bloody-nosed beetle 86
bombardier beetles 44
Brazilian diving beetle 122
bumblebee rove beetle 108
bumblebees 74, 108
burying beetles 100, 122

C
camouflage 30, 38, 76–77, 105
cantharidin 37
cardinal beetles 37
carpet beetle 10
carrion 21, 90, 99
carrion beetles 21
caterpillar hunter 41
cave beetle 102
caves 96, 102
cellar beetle 95
chafer beetles 63, 73, 74, 77
chemical scents 65, 94
chemicals
　for ants 49, 101
　for attracting mates 59, 65
　for defence 27, 36, 44, 69, 86, 90, 91
cicada parasite beetle 59

cockchafer 63
coconut hispine 84
Coleoptera 6
colonies, ant 49
Colorado potato beetle 85
colour change 56
colours 8, 30–31
common claybank tiger beetle 43
common eastern firefly 78
communication 22, 67, 81
conical fungus beetle 36
conservation 122–123
crops 10, 53, 84, 85, 92, 114

D
dead-nettle leaf beetle 31
death-watch beetle 81
decaying matter 20, 21, 27, 48, 51, 83, 100
defence 27, 36, 44, 69, 76–77, 82, 86, 90, 91
deserts 96, 120
devil's coach-horse 90
diet 10–11
digging 48
diving beetles 71
dogbane beetle 10
drugstore beetle 107
dung 48, 50, 55, 96, 108
dung beetles 8, 48, 50, 55
dung tunneller beetle 48

E
eggs 7, 11, 12, 48, 82
Egyptians, ancient 9, 50
elm bark beetle 33
evolution 7, 70
exoskeleton 15
eyes 7, 89

F
false blister beetle 8
featherwing beetle 46
feeding 10–11
fields and meadows 42–67
fighting 7, 16, 17, 23, 25, 26, 34, 51, 55, 62, 80, 118
fighting tortoise beetle 118
fire beetles 116
fireflies 8, 78
flat beetle 48

flat clown beetle 20
flea beetles 66
flightless beetles 79
flower beetles 62, 93
fog-basking beetle 120
foul-tasting/smelling chemicals 27, 36, 69, 86, 90, 91
frog-legged beetle 25
fungi 19, 61, 80
fungus beetles 27, 36, 80

G
gardens 68
giraffe-necked weevil 28
glands 94
globe scarab beetle 58
glow-worm 57
golden scarab beetle 15
golden tortoise beetle 56
golden-green pot beetle 60
Goliath beetle 51
grain weevil 114
Grant's stag beetle 23
great diving beetle 71
green-footed peacock beetle 115
green tortoise beetle 76
ground beetles 11, 41, 44, 49, 98, 101, 115
grubs 7, 11

H
habitat loss 122
habitats 14, 42, 68, 96, 122, 123
hairs 6, 46, 52, 54, 65, 71, 72, 76, 83, 103, 108, 109, 121
harlequin beetle 26
harlequin ladybird 8
harsh habitats 96–121
hazelnut weevil 11
headlight beetle 24
Helm's stag beetle 122
Hercules beetle 16
Himalayan burying beetle 100
homes, human 95, 99, 103, 121
horned fungus beetle 80
horns 16, 34, 51, 55, 80
house longhorn 103
hydrogen peroxide 44
hydroquinone 44

I
infrared light 116
introduced species 41, 52, 87, 92, 99
ironclad beetle 111

J
Japanese beetle 12–13
jaws 7, 11, 17, 23, 97
jewel beetles 65, 75
June beetles 72
juvenile hormone 13

L
lacewings 70
ladybirds 8, 30, 69
larvae 7, 10, 11, 12–13
legs, toothed 15, 20
light-producing chemicals 24, 57
long-snouted weevil 29
longhorn beetles 39, 40, 52, 83, 103
looping flight 78

M
maggots 7
Manticore beetle 97
mates, attracting 38, 57, 59, 62, 81, 83
Maybugs 63
mealybug destroyer 92
mealybugs 68, 92
metallic beetles 17, 21, 31, 41, 58, 62, 66, 75, 115
metallic weevil 32
metamorphosis 12–13
millipedes 35
mimicry 30, 35, 47, 49, 74, 101, 108
Minotaur beetle 55
mole beetle 40
moulds 107
museum beetle 121
museum specimens 123
mushroom rove beetle 61
musk beetle 94

N
narrow grass beetle 45
nectar 8, 42, 82, 91
net-winged beetles 70, 91
nodding contests 28
northern dune tiger beetle 105
number of species 9, 14

O
oil beetles 31

P
palm weevil 87
Parallelomorphus laevigatus 123

parks and gardens 68–95
patterns 6, 8, 30, 31, 64, 76–7
perfumes 94
pest control 8, 41, 68, 69, 92
pests 10, 84, 85, 87, 99, 113, 114, 117
pharmacies 107
pheromones 65
pie-dish beetle 112
pine chafer 77
pine weevil 76
playing dead 111
poison arrow beetle 106
pollination 8
pollution 122
poo 60, 84, 106
pot beetles 60
predators, warning/confusing 30, 31, 32, 36, 37, 56, 57, 69
protected status 122
pupae 12, 13

R
rainbow stag beetle 17
rainforests, tropical 14
red flour beetle 117
reed beetle 119
reflex bleeding 86
rhinoceros beetle 9, 34
rice hispa 53
riverbeds 77
root thatch 42
rose chafer 73
rose oxide 94
rove beetles 61, 90, 108

S
sacred scarab 50
sago worms 87
San people 106
sand 49, 77, 98
sand beetle 98
sand ground beetle 49
scales 6, 31, 32, 72, 76, 121
scarab beetles 9, 15, 50, 58
scents 65, 94
scorpion longhorn 39
sea lavender weevil 104
seven-spot ladybird 69
sightless beetles 102
skin irritation 31
slender long-horned beetle 47
smooth spider beetle 79
snail-killer beetle 67
snouts 11, 29, 88, 114
sound production 22, 67, 81

speckled oil beetle 82
spider beetles 79
spines 53, 56
spotted fungus beetle 27
squirting 44
stag beetles 17, 23, 122
starburst chafer 64
striped cucumber beetle 10
sunburst diving beetle 77
swimming 71, 89

T
ten-lined June beetle 72
thick-legged flower beetle 62
thistle weevil 54
tiger beetles 7, 43, 97, 105
timberman 38
titan longhorn 18
tortoise beetles 56, 76, 118
toxins 37, 69, 82, 86, 91, 106
trilobite beetle 35
triungulins 82, 110
tufted jewel beetle 65
tumbling flower beetle 93
twenty-two-spot ladybird 8

U
underground habitats 96
undertaker beetle 100

V
venom 39
violin beetle 19

W
warning signs/colours 30–31, 37, 69, 86
wasp nest beetle 110
wasps 30, 110
water beetles 77, 122
water
  collecting 120, 112
  living in/under 71, 77, 89, 104, 113, 119
weevils 8, 11, 28–29, 32, 54, 87, 88, 104, 114
wharf borer 113
whirligig beetles 89
willow flea beetle 66
wingless beetles 40, 95, 102
woods and forests 14–41
woodworm beetles 81
woolly bears 121

Y
yeast 107

Project editor Srijani Ganguly
Senior art editor Roohi Rais
Project art editor Bhagyashree Nayak
Art editors Debjyoti Mukherjee, Mitravinda VK
Pre-production designer Dheeraj Singh
Pre-production image editor Vikram Singh
Senior picture researcher Sakshi Saluja
Senior jackets art editor Rashika Kachroo
Managing editor Roohi Sehgal
Managing art editors Diane Peyton Jones, Ivy Sengupta
Production editor Gillian Reid
Production controller Joss Moore
Associate publisher Gemma Farr
India creative head Malavika Talukder
Art director Mabel Chan

Editorial consultant Selina Wood

First published in Great Britain in 2026 by
Dorling Kindersley Limited
20 Vauxhall Bridge Road,
London SW1V 2SA

The authorised representative in the EEA is
Dorling Kindersley Verlag GmbH. Arnulfstr. 124,
80636 Munich, Germany

Copyright © 2026 Dorling Kindersley Limited
A Penguin Random House Company
10 9 8 7 6 5 4 3 2 1
001–345735–April/2026

All rights reserved.
No part of this publication may be reproduced, stored in or introduced into a retrieval system, or transmitted, in any form, or by any means (electronic, mechanical, photocopying, recording, or otherwise), without the prior written permission of the copyright owner.
No part of this publication may be used or reproduced in any manner for the purpose of training artificial intelligence technologies or systems. In accordance with Article 4(3) of the DSM Directive 2019/790, DK expressly reserves this work from the text and data mining exception.

A CIP catalogue record for this book
is available from the British Library.
ISBN: 978-0-2417-2530-6

Printed and bound in China

www.dk.com

This book was made with Forest Stewardship Council™ certified paper – one small step in DK's commitment to a sustainable future.
Learn more at www.dk.com/uk/information/sustainability

About the author:
Richard Jones has been interested in insects, nature, and the environment since childhood, exploring the rivers, hills, and woods of Sussex in England where he grew up. He now carries out ecological surveys and writes about insects.

DK would like to thank:
Radhika Haswani for editorial support; Samrajkumar S for picture research assistance; Jonathan Melmoth for proofreading; Helen Peters for the index; Daniel Long for the feature illustrations; and Angela Rizza for the pattern and cover illustrations.

The publisher would like to thank the following for their kind permission to reproduce their photographs. (Key: a-above; b-below/bottom; c-centre; f-far; l-left; r-right; t-top)

2 Dreamstime.com: Palex66. 3 Dreamstime.com: Alslutsky. 5 Overberg Renosterveld Trust: Odette Curtis-Scott (br). 6 Alamy Stock Photo: ImageBROKER.com / A. Skonieczny (crb). Dreamstime.com: O2beat (bc). 7 Alamy Stock Photo: Nature Picture Library / Alex Hyde (br); Yon Marsh Natural History (tl); Dmitry Ponomarev: (cr). 8–9 Getty Images: Moment / Valter Jacinto (tc). 8 Adobe Stock: Alexey Protasov (bc). Dreamstime.com: Alslutsky (clb). 9 Dreamstime.com: Tanialerro. Getty Images: Hulton Archive / Heritage Images (cra). Shutterstock.com: Mark Brandon (b). 10 Alamy Stock Photo: Gerry Bishop (tl). Bugwood.org: Whitney Cranshaw, Colorado State University (br). naturepl.com: Adrian Davies (cra). 11 Alamy Stock Photo: FLPA (b); Jürgen Kottmann (tc). 12 Alamy Stock Photo: Daniel Borzynski (br). USDA- Animal and Plant Health Inspection Service: (ca). 12–13 Alamy Stock Photo: Dembinsky Photo Associates / Skip Moody (tc/leaf). Dreamstime.com: Paul Reeves (tc). 13 Alamy Stock Photo: Grant Heilman Photography / Runk / Schoenberger (bc). 15 Science Photo Library: Natural History Museum, London. 16 Fotolia: Eric Isselee (b). 17 Adobe Stock: Sabatora. 18 Alamy Stock Photo: The Natural History Museum, London (r). 19 Shutterstock.com: Vince Adam. 20 Dreamstime.com: Cosmin Manci (tl). 21 Shutterstock.com: Kawin Jiaranaisakul. 22 Alamy Stock Photo: Melinda Fawver. 23 Shutterstock.com: R. Maximiliane. 24 Alamy Stock Photo: Nature Picture Library / Kim Taylor. 25 Alamy Stock Photo: Biosphoto / Frank Deschandol & Philippe Sabine. 26 Alamy Stock Photo: Magica. 27 Nicky Bay. 28 Alamy Stock Photo: Nature Picture Library / Kim Taylor (r). 29 Alamy Stock Photo: Biosphoto / Frank Deschandol & Philippe Sabine. 30 Alamy Stock Photo: Science Photo Library. Biosphoto: Michel Gunther (bl, br). 31 Dreamstime.com: Alslutsky (cr); Ian Wilson (tl); Michal Fuglevic (bl). 32 André De Kesel. 33 www.kaefer-der-welt.de. 34 Dreamstime.com: Karel Stipek. 35 Shutterstock.com: Jaiman Taip (r). 36 Alamy Stock Photo: Minden Pictures / Piotr Naskrecki. 37 Nagy Sándor m&m. 38 Milan Lovětínsk. 39 Arystene Nicodemo. 40 Michel Candel. 41 Getty Images / iStock: Wirestock. 43 Aaron Hunt. 44 Alamy Stock Photo: Nature Picture Library / Alex Hyde (l). 45 www.kaefer-der-welt.de. 46 Derek Binns. 47 E. Christina Butler. 48 Alamy Stock Photo: Nature / Piemags (tl). Shutterstock.com: Ferenc Speder (br). 49 Alamy Stock Photo: Peter Yeeles (br). Getty Images: Corbis / Paul Starosta (br). naturepl.com: Nick Upton (tl). 50 Adobe Stock: Holger T.K.. 51 Science Photo Library: Natural History Museum, London. 52 Getty Images / iStock: Zhikun Sun. 53 Dreamstime.com: Alslutsky. 54 Shutterstock.com: Alslutsky. 55 Alamy Stock Photo: Nature Picture Library / Kim Taylor (x2). 56 Getty Images / iStock: Arriyawan (t). 57 Alamy Stock Photo: Nature Photographers Ltd / Paul R. Sterry. 58 naturepl.com: Gil Wizen (b). 59 Shutterstock.com: Wright Out There. 60 Adobe Stock: Lothar Lenz. 61 Nikolai Vladimirov. 62 Dreamstime.com: Henk Wallays. 63 Alamy Stock Photo: Nigel Cattlin. 64 Vinicius Ferreira. 65 Odette Curtis-Scott, Overberg Renosterveld Trust. 66 Dreamstime.com: Alslutsky (bl). 67 Alamy Stock Photo: Blickwinkel / H. Bellmann / F. Hecker. 69 Alamy Stock Photo: Larry Doherty. 70 CC by 4.0 Manaaki Whenua - Landcare Research 2025: Leanne Elder. 71 Alamy Stock Photo: Nature Picture Library / Jan Hamrsky (b). 72 Getty Images / iStock: Gypsy Picture Show. 73 Alamy Stock Photo: Nature Picture Library / Paul Harcourt Davies (t). 74 Shutterstock.com: Vblinov. 75 Shutterstock.com: Isen Stocker. 76 Dreamstime.com: Digitalimagined (cl); Prillfoto (bl). Shutterstock.com: Alslutsky (tr). 77 Dreamstime.com: Mitya Chernov (b). naturepl.com: Suzi Eszterhas (tr). 78 Alamy Stock Photo: Grant Heilman Photography / Runk / Schoenberger. 79 naturepl.com: Photo Ark / Joel Sartore. 80 naturepl.com: Gil Wizen. 81 Gilles San Martin. 82 Nikola Rahme. 83 Dreamstime.com: Jmrocek. 84 Chien C. Lee. 85 Shutterstock.com: Holger Kirk (t). 86 Alamy Stock Photo: www.pqpictures.co.uk. 87 Alamy Stock Photo: Biosphoto / Jean-Claude Carton. 88 Alamy Stock Photo: Nature Picture Library / Andy Sands. 89 naturepl.com: Will Watson. 90 Dreamstime.com: Maciej Olszewski. 91 Judy Gallagher. 92 Gilles San Martin. 93 John Eichler. 94 Dreamstime.com: Viter8. 95 Depositphotos Inc: Imagebrokermicrostock (x2). 97 naturepl.com: Piotr Naskrecki (b). 98 Dreamstime.com: Rasmus Nielsen. 99 Getty Images / iStock: Tomasz Klejdysz. 100 Fan Gao. 101 Alamy Stock Photo: Nature Picture Library / MYN / Piotr Naskrecki. 102 naturepl.com: Alex Hyde. 103 Shutterstock.com: Alslutsky. 104 www.kaefer-der-welt.de. 105 Alamy Stock Photo: Blickwinkel / Bellmann. 106 Alamy Stock Photo: Nature / Piemags. 107 www.kaefer-der-welt.de. 108 Alamy Stock Photo: Nature Photographers Ltd / Paul R. Sterry. 109 Alamy Stock Photo: Imagebroker.com / Hans Lang (t). 110 Rob Coleman. 111 Daniel Sanabria Quirós. 112 Minden Pictures: Martin Withers. 113 Shutterstock.com: Alslutsky. 114 Shutterstock.com: Tomasz Klejdysz (x2). 115 Alamy Stock Photo: Blickwinkel / H. Bellmann / F. Hecker. 116 www.kaefer-der-welt.de. 117 Dreamstime.com: Janny739 (b). 118 Nick Volpe. 119 Alamy Stock Photo: Blickwinkel / Hecker. 120 Alamy Stock Photo: Minden Pictures / Michael & Patricia Fogden. 121 www.kaefer-der-welt.de. 122 Alamy Stock Photo: Anton Sorokin (tr); The Natural History Museum, London (bl). Brett Cortesi: (tl). 123 Charcos Companhia Association: (tr). Getty Images / iStock: Alexey Protasov (c).

Cover images: Front: Dreamstime.com: Alslutsky; Back: Dreamstime.com: Viter8 ca; Getty Images / iStock: Wirestock cra; Shutterstock.com: R. Maximiliane cla; Spine: Dreamstime.com: Alslutsky